CEO From Home

Run a Successful Business On Your Terms

CEO From Home

Run a Successful Business
On Your Terms

Jennifer Morehead & Heather Sallee

BUSINESS
BOOKS

Winchester, UK
Washington, USA

JOHN HUNT PUBLISHING

First published by Business Books, 2022
Business Books is an imprint of John Hunt Publishing Ltd., No. 3 East St., Alresford,
Hampshire SO24 9EE, UK
office@jhpbooks.com
www.johnhuntpublishing.com
www.johnhuntpublishing.com/business-books

For distributor details and how to order please visit the 'Ordering' section on our website.

ISBN: 978 1 78904 787 5
978 1 78904 788 2 (ebook)
Library of Congress Control Number: 2020951005

Design: Stuart Davies

UK: Printed and bound by CPI Group (UK) Ltd, Croydon, CR0 4YY
Printed in North America by CPI GPS partners

We operate a distinctive and ethical publishing philosophy in
all areas of our business, from our global network of authors to
production and worldwide distribution.

Contents

Previous Books:

Make Your Business Social
Chambers, Morehead, Sallee
Business Expert Press, 2020
ISBN: 978-1-95253-800-1

Make Your Nonprofit Social
Chambers, Morehead, Sallee
Business Expert Press, 2020
ISBN: 978-1-95253-864-3

"Whether you think you can, or you think you can't – you're right."
Henry Ford

Jennifer Morehead: To my grandmother Dorothy for inspiring my love of writing. And to my parents Roger and Jan for inspiring my love of entrepreneurship.

Heather Sallee: To my husband for his unwavering support when it comes to my business and who is always ready to listen as I bounce ideas off of him. And to my kids who are a huge reason why I work from home, thanks for putting up with my odd hours.

Introduction

Congratulations on wanting to start or acquire a business that you can run from home. There are massive benefits, including flexibility over your time and an ability to stay in the game on your own terms. By reading this book you are quickly on your way to staying nimble in your field while being close to home, which we would argue is the best way to achieve that elusive balance between work and life outside of it.

There are many reasons that we find ourselves meeting together on these pages. You could be any gender, come from any industry background, and be of any age. You could have worked in the corporate world for 25 years or be fresh out of college. Whatever your reasons, we are happy you are here. Running a business from home isn't for everyone, but with the right alignment of your motivations, skills, and tools in place, it can work for you.

You aren't alone in this quest. Approximately 69 percent of businesses now start in the home. After more than three and a half years, nearly 59 percent are still operating from home.[1] And don't let the hoodie-wearing, college drop-out, twenty something fool you about entrepreneurship, as it truly can start at any age. The average age that people start a business is actually 42 years old, and 60 percent of business owners are between the ages of 40 and 60 years old.[2] Millennial business owners operate 12 percent of all businesses and the rest are owned by people 60 years and older.[3]

By way of introduction, Jennifer Morehead has a background in sales and marketing and founded Salesboxer, which offers social media and marketing support to local businesses throughout the country. Heather Sallee's background is in content creation. She worked as a content creator and an independent contractor for Salesboxer and purchased the business ten years after its inception. The two of us as co-workers and then one founding CEO to an acquiring CEO have unique perspectives on working together and running a business from home. In addition to her expertise as a founding and selling entrepreneur, Jennifer Morehead is the CEO of Flex HR, a human resources outsourcing company. The strategies developed at Flex HR and within this book help entrepreneurs run their business from an office or from home while effectively managing their largest asset: their people.

We will bring you all of the lessons we have learned, researched, and observed. We will also bring you lessons from CEOs working from home in various industries and in different capacities. There are so many different ways to be a CEO from home.

A Note on COVID

Full disclosure, this book was written during the beginning of the COVID pandemic, where the lines between many types of work were greatly blurred. Beyond the heroic healthcare and essential workers who continued their work in person, many were forced to work from home. From top-level corporate CEOs to nationally recognized broadcast journalists, to customer service representatives, people quickly transformed their homes into working spaces.

People started to reconsider their own productivity at home as they removed the commute and time at the water cooler at the office. They discovered that in using the connection tools afforded by technology, they could successfully make advances in their field, run a successful team, and grow a business. While video conferencing and ubiquitous email and phone-based office spaces started the push to work and better-managed time from home, the COVID crisis pushed many more in that direction. So if you are a current CEO coming to this book for advice on running your business from home after COVID has brought your team to their individual homes and kept them there indefinitely, we welcome you as well.

What Our Book Has to Offer

As mentioned before, technology has allowed for many blurred lines in our economy, in terms of where you work. Now in a post-COVID world these lines become even more blurred when considering running a business from home. We welcome any and all readers to our pages; however, this book will specifically explore starting, acquiring, and running a company from home. You can also pick up some great points about starting a side hustle if that's your goal.

We are passionate about the benefits of owning your own business. There is a huge difference between earning a paycheck as an employee and owning equity in the work that you are pursuing. After all, you have the ability to pass down the business to a family member or friend, or sell the business with a payout that takes you beyond your bi-weekly checks.

We hear from a lot of people who want to own the work they do, both for financial stability and the ability to design work around their time. We will identify the different ways you can own what you do, through three different CEO types, and we would argue most don't require 80 hours a week. We will provide the tips, sources, and shortcuts to ensure that you can run your own business very much within the time that you have available. While our advice is fairly evergreen you might find that in time some of the websites we refer to will have come and gone. This happens, so don't get distracted but follow the very basis of our advice to get going.

We will offer insights for all kinds of CEOs from home, from those who want to start the next technology unicorn to those running a commercial real estate empire, to those dominating the gig economy. There have never been more options. We are going to roll up our sleeves and get started on a journey that will help each of you achieve success and fulfillment through your work at home.

Introduction Key Takeaways

After reading this chapter, what should you understand?

1. Start to identify your motivations for being a CEO from home.
2. There is a stronger urgency for running a business from home in a post-COVID world.
3. A CEO from home can define their work around the time they have available.
4. The line can be blurred between a side hustle and a true company and is up to you to define.

Endnotes

1 Anita Campbell. "69 Percent of U.S. Entrepreneurs Start Their Businesses at Home." Accessed October 7, 2020. https://smallbiztrends.com/2013/07/home-based-busi nesses-startup.html

2 Dragomir Simovic. "39 Entrepreneur Statistics You Need to Know in 2020." Accessed October 7, 2020. https:// www.smallbizgenius.net/by-the-numbers/entrepreneur-statistics/#gref

3 "2020 Small Business Trends." Accessed October 7, 2020. https://www.guidantfinancial.com/small-business-trends/

Chapter 1

Find Your CEO Type

Welcome to the start of your journey to becoming a CEO from home. There is so much opportunity in being your own boss and it has never been easier in terms of the technology that allows each of us to do purposeful and interesting work on our own terms, from a home office. You might be coming to these pages wanting to set up a business, to buy a business, or to establish or continue the work of your company with a virtual office set-up. In following our suggestions, you will ensure ownership over your work from home and, in turn, your life. We will give you the right ways to think about which CEO type you are and what business works for you, and then we will take you through the actual steps to get started to effectively run a virtual business.

While becoming your own boss from home is both an art and a science, we will guide you through the more black and white elements, so that you can add the creative side that will make your company and journey unique. We will go through the three different CEO types, the industries that work best for each type, and provide ideas on funding, finding good people, marketing, sales, and growth. We will talk about strategies for developing a good culture in a virtual setting. You can use our book with its sequential chapters, or refer to it as a workbook, referring to sections as you need them. More than anything, we will get you to actually start on your journey, which is the hardest and most important part.

Think of the last proverbial cocktail party you attended, whether it was in person or over Zoom, and ask yourself how you felt coming away from your time with others in terms of what you do professionally. It's a cliched challenge for a reason, because it creates that impetus for change. If you are looking for that change, and maybe you've been looking for some time, congratulations on taking a huge step that will involve starting a new business, side hustle, or running an existing business from home.

Maybe you are just out of college and have dreamed of becoming an entrepreneur. Perhaps you've spent too many nights in hotels traveling for a job you don't like anymore. Or you want to contribute at a higher level in your industry and have ownership in what you do. Maybe you are the CEO of a current business that was sent home for months on end from the COVID pandemic and you want to work virtually from now on. Look no further, as this is a straightforward journey to becoming an effective CEO from home.

What Do You Want from This Experience?

Let's begin identifying your CEO type with a bit of a therapy session. You can pretend you are sprawled on the sofa and speaking with your therapist for the moment. There are four elements that will go into what CEO type you choose and they are somewhat related: time capacity, interests, motivations, and long-term goals.

Before you move forward with a CEO type, you should start by examining your capacity for the work. While your financial capacity is important too, we will address that later. Let's start with your time capacity. The answer to these questions will help determine what kind of business you want to start and what your goals should be.

- Are you looking to work fewer hours so that you can spend more time with family or friends?
- Do you want to work more hours on a dream business that you want to bring to life?
- How many hours a week do you want to work?
- Do you have a big idea that you've been dying to try out

in the marketplace, but never had the time?

- Do you want a side hustle that allows you to stay engaged while having an incredibly flexible lifestyle?

For example, if you want to work fewer hours than the 50-hour-a-week desk job with the hour-long commute, you might not want to start a business thinking that you will scale quickly and become a major player in the marketplace. That will lead to working even longer hours than the job you are leaving. Instead, you would want to think differently and perhaps find a niche and make more manageable goals. In this case, bigger might not be better for you.

On the other hand, maybe the job you are in hasn't challenged you enough. Maybe the reason you're looking to start your own business from home is that you want to build something of your own, in which you can be proud. If that's the case, you might not mind longer hours and you may want to think big. Your goals will be loftier, and you'll need to acquire more resources, capital, and make more hires up front.

Next, you need to examine your interests. You're starting a business, not a hobby, so it needs to be something you can commit to. What are you knowledgeable about or interested in? If you wouldn't use or buy the product or service your company is there to solve, your ambition will only get you so far. Eventually, it will feel like you're back in the grind.

Draw a picture of the ideal life you dream of with your new business.

- What types of business are you interested in running?
- What are your qualifications and experience?
- Would you want to run a business with a product or service?
- Do you want your business to focus on selling to consumers or other businesses?

Take some time to identify what you want. In order for the leap to owning your own business to be worth it, you need to make sure you are aligning your goals according to what you authentically want. You may need to sacrifice some of these wants a little along the way, but ultimately you should be setting yourself up for something sustainable and rewarding.

Third, and this is very much related to your time capacity and interests, let's look at your motivations for being a CEO from home. Be honest and authentic with yourself about your intentions for wanting this work lifestyle. We have outlined a few motivations that could be behind your desire to run a business from home. Do any of these resonate?

Motivations for Being a CEO from Home	
Autonomy	Money
Flexibility	Lifestyle
Time at Home	Status
Ability to Follow Passions	Work/Life Balance
Skill Mastery	Lifelong Dream of Entrepreneurship

The motivations above are by no means an exhaustive list, but they get you started in thinking about why it is that you want to take the leap. Identify which motivations might be leading you down this path. You will use these motivations throughout the book to understand what makes you tick and what can lead to the most successful outcome in your journey as a CEO from home.

In terms of what other entrepreneurs say about motivations, 26 percent say their biggest motivation for starting their own business was the idea of being their own boss.[1] Gallup has found that 54 percent of office workers would leave their job if they could have one with more flexibility,[2] which is a real motivation when starting a business or thinking of taking an existing business to a fully virtual or near-virtual status. *Entrepreneur* magazine and website offers these top five motivations for people starting their own business: money, flexibility, control, working with people that you choose, and legacy.[3]

But you also have to think authentically about if you are well suited for running a business from home. Jim Anderson, of LeadDog Consulting, says the first part of starting a home-based business is recognizing what kind of personality you have. If you need someone else to give you that structure, or if you are a procrastinator, a home office is probably not the best thing for you.[4]

Finally, in addition to your time capacity, interests and motivations, we want you to think about what your work should offer in terms of tangible long-term outcomes. What, beyond the day-to-day grind, do you want from your work? What are your goals, personally and professionally, for the next five years? For the next ten years?

When you can put more meaning behind your work, it becomes easier to excel. Check out some potential long-term goals:

- An expertise to write, teach, or join a board
- A foray into philanthropic work
- An ability to pass along the business to friends or family
- An ability to have an exit and large cash payout

You can really dream here. These meaningful and exciting long-term goals won't happen without you forming some idea of what it is you want to have happen and then breaking it down into smaller goals. We encourage you to look thoroughly into your time capacity, interests, motivations, and long-term goals. It becomes very powerful when you authentically align these elements.

The Three CEO Types

Too much of life is complicated, so we are going to help you get started on your journey with something really simple. You can choose between three different CEO types. There are many shades of gray within these three types, but in the interest of maintaining simplicity, we will present you with our thought process, which will help us categorize different concepts throughout the book. Within each of these three CEO types there is a time commitment spectrum that we refer to as side hustle, absentee owner and active owner.

Someone running a side hustle might work as few as 5–10 hours per week. It's entirely possible to run a business as a side hustle if you are smart about your time and outsource a lot. The absentee owner might work 20–35 hours per week and is disciplined with their time and good at delegating and working with independent-minded employees and consultants. Make no mistake, the side hustle CEO and absentee owner CEO are both still very much involved in the business; however, they are able to divide and delegate to efficiently manage their time. As a society, we are most familiar with an active owner CEO. He or she may operate a business with more weekly hourly needs or the active owner might want to put stronger growth objectives on the business. An active owner CEO is working anywhere from 35 hours per week or more.

Between a time commitment that we have categorized above as side hustle, active and absentee, there are three CEO types:

- **Residual income CEO.** The CEO is running multiple residual income streams that add up together to form an annual income. They are buying or creating an asset from which they can passively earn an income.
- **Gig owner CEO.** The CEO has a specialty and hires others to work for them within that specialty. In most cases, they are running a business that offers one to a few services.

- **Traditional owner CEO.** The CEO is managing products or services that they have created or acquired. In most cases, they are running a business with a complex set of services or products.

Let's refer back to the challenge from the beginning of our book when we asked about how you felt in the last cocktail party you attended, talking about what you do. Where do you want to be now on the chart?

	Side Hustle Working 5–10 hours per week	Absentee Working 20–35 hours per week	Active Working 35+ hours per week
Residual Income CEO Managing an asset with passive income.			
Gig Owner CEO Running a business with one to a few services.			
Traditional Owner CEO Running a business with a complex set of services or products.			

As with most things in life, there is oftentimes a trade-off between money and time. We realize this isn't the end-all in working from home as the boss but it provides a simplistic framework.

Let's give some examples. An online influencer might be considered a residual income CEO. She might be doing it full time as an absentee owner, but she has created her own asset and is now making passive income from it. The influencer might start up a business that offers jewelry or clothes, and in this way moves to an active traditional owner CEO. Another example of an absentee owner residual income CEO is someone who has invested in an apartment complex with 30 units. He has hired a project manager but is also very much involved and looking at the next opportunity.

Perhaps it's someone who has started an SEO business. You could classify this as a gig owner CEO. She is able to hire five independent contractors and work as an absentee owner creating a brand, strategy, and customer portfolio for her business. Maybe it's a lawyer who is able to offer a legal service such as real estate law or estate law and he's able to do it as an absentee or active gig owner CEO.

You might have someone who has worked in human resources for his entire career. He wants more flexibility as he is at retirement age, but he wants to still put his knowledge and skills to use. So he sets up a consulting side hustle business where he can work 5–10 hours per week. He would be considered a side hustle gig owner CEO, as he has made an asset of his specified knowledge and expertise.

Then there is someone who might be running a textile business with multiple product offerings. Or an entrepreneur who is running her own public relations business. Another person might be running a medical billing company with ten employees who all work virtually. All three could be active, traditional owner CEOs or because they have a certain team, could reduce hours over time to be an absentee owner.

Let's break down some of the jargon we hear about entrepreneurship in the news, such as lifestyle business, small company, or startup. A side hustle or absentee owner could qualify as running what is sometimes called a lifestyle business. This means the side hustle or absentee owner is either able to manage the business with reduced hours per week or they are able to outsource the day-to-day functions of the business and work in a strategic role. An active or absentee owner can run what is referred to as a small business, and it maintains a steady growth trajectory. Finally, a startup is what might be covered in the *Wall Street Journal*, where an entrepreneur or team created a business and it scaled, or grew, quickly. Sometimes when the startup is extraordinarily successful it's referred to as a unicorn.

We talked about motivations and long-term goals before and now they start coming into play. You want to think about your life when the business is humming along. A startup is sexy, exciting, usually gets more press, and in its ideal state will grow quickly. It does usually require the extra steps of selling your concept to investors and meeting their expectations on at least a quarterly and annual basis. A small business will ideally allow for expected time and money goals to be met and could help achieve those long-term goals that you identified. A lifestyle business will usually grow more slowly but if you create or buy it correctly, it should be lower in risk and time commitments.

Next, in the interest of time because we know everyone is busy, we are going to give you the key points of this book. These will get you ready for the detail to follow.

1. Determine your time capacity, interests, motivations and long-term goals for being a CEO from home.
2. Decide which of the three types of CEOs you are: the residual income CEO, the gig owner CEO, or the traditional owner CEO.
3. Determine your weekly hourly commitment to work and if you want to be a side hustle owner, absentee owner or active owner.
4. Pick the right industry for your CEO type. We advise buying a company that already exists.
5. Beware of money traps like expensive web development and legal fees.

6. Find a niche with a following.
7. Identify a pain point that you want to solve and roadblocks to getting started.
8. Market research is key to understanding how to sell your product or service.
9. For product testing, discover ways to get people to interact, such as offering the product for free in the beginning.
10. Pick your name and use keywords that make it easier for people to find you.
11. Make sure your logo showcases who you are and what you do.
12. Your marketing activities will most likely start with paid lead sources, public relations, social media, email marketing, and guerrilla marketing tactics.
13. Sell yourself by being relatable, authentic, and a person of integrity. You represent your brand.
14. Learn to listen to your customers. Ask for their input and feedback in the selling process and take it to heart.
15. Think long-term about building a trusting relationship with your customers when you're selling.
16. You can set up your business on your own without the additional legal fees that so many people think about when they hear a business startup.
17. Be as lean as possible during your first two years to ensure your company's success.
18. Be mindful of the complexity and necessity of a good human resources strategy for your business and don't be afraid to outsource this to experts.
19. Identify the type of talent you need based on authenticity to your company and its vision.
20. Develop a careful interview and assessment process to make sure a candidate is the right fit.
21. Develop a target demographic to attract the most

customers.

22. Consider paid advertising only after you have some customers coming in and can afford it.

23. Use a daily huddle among your management team to communicate effectively and touch base each day.

24. Develop a reliable analytics tool (or two) before your official launch to monitor how your business is doing.

25. There are outward-focused and inward-focused efficiencies that give your business huge advantages.

26. Develop partnerships and strategies with the influencers of your audience.

27. Simplify and delegate to make sure that inward-focused operations are running efficiently.

28. Think about the three outcomes of your business, which will be to scale, maintain or pivot, and be prepared for each outcome.

29. Identify the long-term goals of your work and your business so it carries more significance for you.

Executing on Your Idea

The idea for your business is important, but even more critical is how you execute each day. We want you to spend much more time focused on execution, life fit, and talent fit than on coming up with wild ideas for a good business. Remember not to get too caught up in the idea, name, colors of the logo, and other items that are small details in the bigger picture. Execution is everything.

In your business, you will need some combination of operators and strategists. An operator might be more linear in their thinking. They enjoy carefully planning the budgets and making sure everything is consistent and on track. A strategist oftentimes has the big ideas. Their head is in the clouds thinking of the next big thing for the business. There are also hybrid people who are somewhere on the spectrum between operator and strategist.

A successful business has operator and strategist strengths in their management team. More casually, if you are a side hustle or absentee owner, you might want these strengths in a spouse, significant other, or friend. In the beginning, if you know that you fall on one side of the spectrum more than the other, you should think about bringing on a partner, an influential board member, or hiring your first person with complementary strengths. Remembering the dichotomy between operator and strategist is important when considering how you run your business.

Overcoming Obstacles

You will want to be aware of the roadblocks that might stop you before getting started on your journey. The most common roadblock is a lack of funding.[5] Money can be a real limitation. Take a good look at your financial situation. Chances are, unless you've been saving for your business for a while, you will need some kind of outside funding or you will need to pull from funds you've allocated for other areas of your life. If the financial aspect of getting started is the issue you're facing, read on. We will show you how to get the funding you need for your business.

Maybe the roadblock you're facing is time. You can't afford to quit your job and you're not willing to work overtime to make your business happen. If that's the case, you'll need to find an approach that balances flexibility and stability, such as working fewer hours or part time in your main job to give you the time you need.

Another roadblock is not knowing the correct steps to take.[6] It can seem intimidating when you don't know what to do. Keep reading and we will outline all of your necessary next steps to get your business launched.

If the personal roadblock you face is a lack of confidence,

then we suggest you get some support. Running a business is difficult and it can be hard to be your own cheerleader at times. Get your spouse or significant other, family, and friends behind you so that when the going gets tough you can keep going. Become more comfortable in sharing details about the business you are planning to run, as anyone can be a potential partner or referral.

Whatever the roadblocks you might face, identify them and figure out a way to overcome them. You can get there, just like countless others before you.

Just Start Already

We encourage you to just get started. Let's turn to Warren Buffett, the great investor and owner of Berkshire Hathaway, for some advice on what separates the doers from the dreamers. He suggests that incredibly successfully people say no to almost everything. Buffett maintains that you should also invest in your communication skills and make sure both written and verbal skills are top notch. Buffett recommends surrounding yourself with friends who challenge and inspire you. And finally, he says that you should aim to go to bed smarter each day. Reading is crucial to knowing more than your competition.[7]

Beyond anything we have discussed in this first chapter, the most important thing to remember is just to start. Don't let perfection be the enemy of done. Here are some very basic tactical tips to getting started:

- Identify your big goal and break it down to smaller steps
- Set up a calendar with a realistic timeline and work backward
- Set up time within your current schedule and make tangible changes in behavior that align with those steps and the larger goal
- Make your goals public, to hold yourself accountable

- Be honest with yourself

You don't have to get everything perfect the first time around and trust us, you won't. Getting each step done is better than making sure everything is done to utter perfection. Your business won't be able to move forward if your perfectionist tendencies hold it back. Be willing to get a little messy when you start. Become accustomed to breaking through those roadblocks as you figure it out and learn along the way.

Chapter 1 Key Takeaways

After reading this chapter, what should you understand?

1. Determine your time capacity, interests, motivations and long-term goals for being a CEO from home.
2. Decide which of the three types of CEOs you are: the residual income CEO, the gig owner CEO, or the traditional owner CEO.
3. Determine your weekly hourly commitment to work and if you want to be a side hustle owner, absentee owner or active owner.
4. Don't let perfection be the enemy of done.

Endnotes

1   Marius Kiniulis. "11 Entrepreneur Statistics You Need To Know." Accessed October 7, 2020. https://www.markinblog. com/entrepreneur-statistics/

2   Kellie Wong. "25 Key Remote Work Statistics for 2020." Accessed October 7, 2020. https://www. business2community.com/human-resources/25-key-remote-work-statistics-for-2020-02299342

3   Larry Alton. "The 5 Motivations That Drive People To Choose Entrepreneurship." Accessed October 7, 2020. https://www.entrepreneur.com/article/249417

4   Tamara Schweitzer. "How to Run a Business From Home."
    Accessed October 7, 2020. https://www.inc.com/ss/how-
    run-business-home

5   Murray Goldstein. "5 roadblocks that keep people from
    opening startups." Accessed May 14, 2020. https://
    www.coxblue.com/5-roadblocks-that-keep-people-from-
    opening-startups-coxnsbw/

6   Murray Goldstein. "5 roadblocks that keep people from
    opening startups." Accessed May 14, 2020. https://
    www.coxblue.com/5-roadblocks-that-keep-people-from-
    opening-startups-coxnsbw/

7   Marcel Schwantes. "Warren Buffett Says 4 Choices in
    Life Separate the Doers From the Dreamers." Accessed
    October 7, 2020. https://www.inc.com/marcel-schwantes/
    warren-buffett-says-4-choices-in-life-separate-doers-from-
    dreamers.html

Chapter 2

Pick an Industry

You have had a moment to think about your motivations, long-term goals, and preference for CEO type. Now we will expand on the three CEO types to offer ideas of business industries for each one. It is by no accident that we are outlining the business industries and CEO types at the beginning, as making these choices correctly is essential for getting started in the right way and picking the correct business. If you misfire here you will struggle in becoming the successful CEO from home that you want to be. Take some time to really think and envision what is authentically good for you.

Business industry is a catch-all phrase that helps categorize companies related by their primary business activities.[1] On Facebook if you are setting up a business page, you need to assign it to a category. If you are putting your business on Google Ads it's called an industry. It can be called a lot of things, but your company's industry allows you to understand growth trends, competition, potential lead sources, and more. Here it will allow you to further narrow down your choices to quickly decide on a business to start or to acquire.

You can start brainstorming by finding a website that features industry categories and scrolling through them. This chapter will allow for you to do some stream of consciousness thinking and other brainstorming to get you closer to your ultimate goal. Don't put the pressure on yourself yet for identifying the exact business that you will run. Instead, give yourself space and time to explore what type of work is right for you.

Again, let's identify our three CEO types:

- **Residual income CEO.** The residual income CEO runs an

asset with a passive income stream. You might even start combining multiple passive income streams that add up together to form a healthy annual income.

- **Gig owner CEO.** The gig owner CEO has a specialty in one or a few services and hires others to work for them within that specialty.
- **Traditional owner CEO.** The traditional owner CEO is managing a more complex set of products and/or services that they have created or acquired.

Choose a Business Industry: Residual Income CEO

Residual, or passive, income is money you make that is not directly tied to your time. Think of the industries that allow you to set up an asset to collect a passive income. They could involve commercial property, transactional website offerings, information products, investing, and more. Large businesses can also grow from the idea of creating multiple assets that collect a passive income, but we can start here with the right industry for a residual income CEO.

Let's explore the commercial property industry first. You will most likely be purchasing a property if you go this route and it is important here, as it is with other business ventures, that you effectively negotiate the purchase price at the onset. We have broken commercial properties into four major subcategories: residential rentals, industrial, office, and retail.

The various types of commercial real estate (sometimes known as CRE) are broken down into three classes: Class A, Class B, and Class C. Every property you evaluate will have its own unique risk and reward, but the class system allows investors to understand their potential return on investment.[2] Generally speaking, the higher the class the higher the value. The property classes are based on the following credentials:

- Property construction year
- Location and access
- Tenant income levels
- Potential or current rental income
- Growth potential
- Amenities
- Appreciation

We have a few tips to decide between the four main commercial property subcategories of residential rentals, industrial, office and retail. Currently, we feel that residential rentals are the safest subcategory of commercial properties. You can invest in apartments, multi-family, and single-family homes within residential rentals. The common thought for rental units is that you can use a property manager if you have 20 or more units. If you are able to efficiently use your time by hiring a property manager and overseeing the work, it becomes a much more time-efficient equation.

Industrial properties will usually be priced at the lowest cost per square foot among these four subcategories of commercial real estate. The companies that come to rent your space might be there for a long time; however, it's very easy for them to find a better deal and move their location, since they aren't consumer facing.

Retail and office buildings will be priced a bit higher than industrial properties per square foot. Pay particular attention to trends and capitalization rate when comparing different properties. The COVID crisis changed where people could work, which has impacted commercial real estate and rentals. City dwellers moved to zoom towns where they could work and enjoy time outdoors.[3] Use trends and your knowledge of the area to inform your decisions.

You can use the property's cap rate to generalize comparison. The cap rate is the rate of return on a real estate property based on the income that is expected. The cap rate is net operating income divided by the property's asset value. So an example would be if you purchased a property for $1,000,000 and it has a net income of $100,000, the cap rate is 10 percent.[4]

Other types of residual income in the commercial property space include farms, RV parks, and parking lots. For any of these commercial properties, you would do an online search for websites that sell these properties and start making calls. We recommend that you do what you know, but if you can't do that, start calling people who are experts and ask questions. We recommend purchasing an existing commercial property where you can see a profit and loss statement so you have historical data. You will negotiate a purchase contract and will want to make sure there isn't a lot of deferred maintenance so that you can make money on the investment.

Following the commercial real estate space, you can also look at purchasing or starting a transactional website. There are online marketplaces for these types of websites, such as Flippa. For example, you can purchase an existing website that makes $1,000 or $2,000 per month and add this to your other assets. You will want to do extensive research to make sure you purchase a legitimate website in this space and that it has some established credibility. Look at the historical data and talk with the current owner of the website to ensure you can continue to make the money that is advertised. If you want to start a transactional website, look at the online marketplaces for ideas on what to start and how much money you can expect to make.

Next, you can look at creating an information source as a residual income opportunity. You could be working as a personal trainer and put together a series of workouts that require a subscription fee. You could put together a series of books that allow you to collect passive income. Or you could put together an online class in an area of your specialty. You could select something in your expertise from many different industries to create an information source that allows you to collect residual income.

Investing is another residual income CEO opportunity. You can become knowledgeable in equity and bond investing and work with the assets that you have to more closely run them and make a salary. You could also invest for a small group of friends and family, for a smaller fee than a bank or financial manager would charge.

These opportunities for a residual income CEO are not an exhaustive list, but they are a start. The essence of a residual income CEO is to passively make money on a given asset. Once you choose or develop the asset, own it, and can generate money from it, you can get started.

Choose a Business Industry: Gig Owner CEO

With a gig owner CEO business type, you are picking an area where you, or a team that you hire, have expertise. We will use the example of the website and marketplace Upwork. Upwork helps employers find all types of independent contractors such as writers who are experts in social media or people who run search engine optimization for companies. Ideas for industries that cater to being a gig owner CEO include administrative support, accounting, customer service, writing, architectural design, and legal work.

To become a gig owner CEO you can start by signing up on a website like Upwork in the specialty that applies to you. In time, you could create a brand and a company that other employers could turn to for hiring just your type of specialty. This works for an infinite group of specialties such as carpentry, handymen, content creation, advertising help, estate planning, and more. You can find additional ideas for industries by going to the generalist websites and scrolling through the types of specialties they provide.

When you are ready to start your gig owner business, you will want to establish yourself as the expert in your field and create the brand. Next, you hire people directly as independent contractors to your business and find a way to attract customers who need your specialists. This type of business has a relatively low barrier to entry, with low risks and costs associated with setting it up. You can also, as always, acquire an existing business.

The essence of a gig owner CEO is to develop a team that can thrive in a given specialty and develop an expertise. Your pitch to the specialists is that you will do their sales and marketing for them and they don't have to rely on a website to get their next gig. Your pitch to the customers is that you only specialize in a certain area and so you will get the job done better.

Choose a Business Industry: Traditional Owner CEO

The sky is the limit for a traditional owner CEO working from home. You could choose a business in fashion, technology, interior design, pet supplies, or from any number of other industries. There are so many businesses that can operate with a smaller workforce or a workforce that is fully remote and you can absolutely manage this from your home. Let's turn to our research to show the best industries for remote work, based on the highest number of remote job openings.[5]

- Information Technology
- Sales
- Healthcare
- Project and Account Management
- Customer Service
- Consulting
- Education
- Marketing
- Human Services
- Translation
- Financial

Regardless of the industry that you choose, you will need to carefully craft a team and a culture that can accommodate a virtual working lifestyle. COVID created an even playing field for traditional and virtual companies alike and, because of the pandemic, we have a lot more ideas about how to successfully run a business virtually. As the leader, you will want to provide your team with stability, identity, social cohesion, and belonging even while working from home.[6]

DJ Haddad is the CEO of Haddad and Partners, a full-service creative agency that works with clients such as Capital One, Citibank, Microsoft, Barclays, and HBO. Haddad is a father of four and employs 65 people through his business. He says, "I am lucky to work with the greatest team on the planet, and somehow we have all become friends and created this amazing chemistry remotely over Microsoft Teams. We have Team chats for everything – book club, employees with kids, employees without kids, competitions, etc. It makes it easy for us to still have fun and have 'water cooler talk' throughout the day."[7]

Online-Only Businesses

Let's take a look at the different types of online-only businesses to show how you can craft these as a residual owner CEO, gig owner CEO, and traditional owner CEO. When we talk about an online-only business some people associate that with the startup unicorns of Silicon Valley like SnapChat and Facebook. In reality, starting something from scratch is very risky and the likelihood that a company reaches unicorn status is low. However, you can start different types of online businesses that when ideated and managed correctly allow you to be the CEO from home that you had envisioned.

The structure of the online-only business really gets into the core of what you will be doing. Online-only businesses usually fall into these five categories or will be a hybrid of a few of them.

1. Community: Within a community model, you will bring people together to your website to achieve a specific goal, whether it is to find love, check in on people, or sell something. Think of Facebook, TikTok, and SnapChat.
2. Ecommerce: An ecommerce model allows people to quickly and easily buy something online. Examples include Amazon and Zappos.
3. Information Platform: These are websites that we go to for information and entertainment, such as newspapers and bloggers online. They hold our attention. Examples include Reddit, HuffPost, Mashable, and TechCrunch.
4. Provider Connection: People are very targeted when they come online. Websites that connect consumers with the providers they are looking for can capitalize on lead generation revenue. Examples include Angie's List and Homefinder.com.
5. Software as a Service: These are websites that help you perform a service for yourself better, faster, and cheaper. The websites have software embedded within them that allows users to easily move through their system. An example here is the behemoth Salesforce.

Finally, and most importantly, you should evaluate the revenue source for your online-only business. No matter how lean your business will be, or how much investor money you raise, you will inevitably need to pay bills. Through evaluating your skills, what you are selling, and the structure of your business, you can determine the best revenue source. Here are some suggestions for revenue sources for your online-only business:

1. Advertising: Selling the attention of people who come to your website. Usually you will be looking at $1–$3 cost per thousand people for an ad to run, so you need to build up a big audience to your site or sell to a niche

audience where you can charge higher rates.

2. Affiliate: Selling the link from your site to a related product. You're looking at 2%–10% of a sale that is made on the site in which you have directed your user.

3. Lead Generation: Selling the information of a user who has willingly given it for a specific provider. You can get anything from $5 to $30 for leads or more, depending on exclusivity and industry.

4. Subscription: Selling a specific product or service that a consumer will agree to pay on a monthly or yearly basis. Prices can vary.

5. Transactional: Selling a product with a quick relationship. The customer comes in, buys something, and leaves. Prices can vary, but you should start with conservative forecasts of 1 to 2% of people who come to your site would buy a product and the number can grow as they become more familiar with you.

You might be a residual income CEO that is establishing the advertising, affiliate, and lead generation models for an online-only business. You might be a gig income CEO with a subscription service for a particular specialty. Or you might be a traditional owner CEO with a subscription or transaction service.

Acquire Your Business

We believe in buying an established business rather than starting your own. Whatever CEO type you want to be and whichever industry you choose, we would strongly recommend purchasing a known company. People think that entrepreneurs are incredibly risk-tolerant, and of course this can be true. However, some of the most successful entrepreneurs are the ones who actually are better at mitigating risks along the way, whether it be from purchasing a known quantity to run with specific skills, or getting just the right investor so that you don't have to put up as much money in the beginning.

Post-COVID-19 Trends

As we discuss industries for your specific CEO type, we would be remiss to not include trends that have come after the wave of COVID. In general, you always want to think deeply about emerging trends. But COVID, and the ensuing global pandemic, created a sea change in consumer behavior. While we don't want to give ideas that are trendy, we feel that it's important to think about what subcategories within broader industries could continue to be strong in a post-COVID world. Here are our ideas:

- Telehealth
- Online education
- Telecommuting
- At-home services such as beauty, eating plans and self-care
- Home and yard improvement
- Virtual reality
- Pets/pet care
- Safety gear and supplies

As an entrepreneur you will want to make sure that your innovation and business are addressing a long-term problem that will still be here three to five years from now and beyond. Dirk Schroeder is the CEO of Updraft Health Innovation Advisors and the Co-Founder of HolaDoctor Inc., a Spanish-language digital health company. Schroeder recommends evaluating a COVID trend by looking at 2019 and earlier and then analyzing how COVID created or amplified the problem. He writes, "For example, the need to care for patients from a distance, a problem solved by telehealth and remote-patient monitoring, certainly existed prior to 2020. What changed with COVID-19 were the widespread stay-at-home orders, more widely available video and home-based technologies and, in the case of telehealth, changes in regulations and reimbursement, which together, have led to a tremendous demand for these services." If you are a COVID-inspired entrepreneur, you will want to ask yourself if there will be a large enough number of customers to grow a business once coronavirus is under control.[8]

As you move along your journey to becoming a CEO from home, you want to be thoughtful and purposeful in making the right choices, especially in the beginning. It is extremely powerful when you are authentic to the type of CEO you want to be and the industry that is most appealing to you.

Chapter 2 Key Takeaways
After reading this chapter, what should you understand?

1. Pick the right industry for your CEO type. We advise buying a company that already exists rather than starting something new.
2. The residual owner CEO can select multiple opportunities such as managing commercial properties, websites, or investments.
3. The gig owner CEO can hire people as independent contractors to run a successful business that specializes in a particular expertise.
4. The traditional owner CEO can choose any number of industries.
5. As an entrepreneur, you should always be mindful of emerging trends.

Endnotes
1   Will Kenton. "Industry." Accessed October 7, 2020. https://www.investopedia.com/terms/i/industry.asp

2   "An Investor's Guide to Commercial Real Estate Building Classes." Accessed September 5, 2020. https://fnrpusa.com/commercial-real-estate-building-classes/

3   Greg Rosalsky. "Zoom Towns and the New Housing Market for the 2 Americas." Accessed October 7, 2020. https://www.npr.org/sections/money/2020/09/08/909680016/zoom-towns-and-the-new-housing-market-for-the-2-americas

4   Robert Schmidt. "What You Should Know About The Cap Rate." Accessed October 7, 2020. https://propertymetrics.com/blog/cap-rate/

5   Christy Williams. "19 Best Remote Work Industries – Top 20 List." Accessed October 7, 2020. https://www.virtualvocations.com/blog/telecommuting-news/2019-best-remote-work-industries/

6   Andrea Alexander, Aaron De Smet, and Mihir Mysore. "Reimagining the Postpandemic Workforce." Accessed October 7, 2020. https://www.mckinsey.com/business-functions/organization/our-insights/reimagining-the-postpandemic-workforce#

7   Elisette Carlson. "10 Tips From CEOs on Working From Home Effectively and Happily." Accessed October 7, 2020. https://www.entrepreneur.com/article/347479

8   Dirk Schroeder. "Turn Your COVID-19 Solution into a Viable Business." Accessed October 7, 2020. https://hbr.org/2020/07/turn-your-COVID-19-solution-into-a-viable-business?registration=success

Chapter 3

Select a Business

Think of all the times you have read the news about an emerging entrepreneur and thought, 'I could have done that.' Or the times you have gone on social media to see a carefree entrepreneur talking about how success feels. Or maybe it's the friends you have known who have gone out on their own. All of those positive profiles of people running a business don't show the ups and downs, because of course they exist. But we encourage you to focus on the excitement, thrill and positivity as you start. Adopting an attitude of cautious optimism will give you a big boost. Gather that energy, along with the CEO type and industry you have chosen, and put it toward selecting the business that you are going to run.

Let's talk about the good news before the bad news. The good news is that 62 percent of US billionaires are self-made, so you are headed in a good direction if money is a motivation. There are more than 25 million Americans who have started or are already running their own business. And more than 78% of small businesses survive their first year.[1]

But why exactly does a business succeed? Patrick Henry, the founder and CEO of QuestFusion, looked to The Ecommerce Genome by Compass report and put together key factors for success:[2]

- Founders are driven by impact, which results in passion and commitment to stay the course
- A flexibility for adjustment, but not constantly adjusting
- Patience and persistence
- A deep connection with the customer's needs
- Willingness to learn, observe, and listen

- Develop the right relationships with mentors
- Leadership with domain specific and general business knowledge

Now for the bad news, which is why businesses don't succeed. Thinking about why businesses don't succeed is entirely relevant when picking one to run. The number one reason why businesses fail, and it happens to 42 percent of them, is that there isn't enough market need. Next, approximately 29 percent of businesses that fail will do so because they run out of money. The third reason, at 23 percent, is more of a management issue, where a business fails due to lack of chemistry between employees and company leaders.[3]

Take these reasons for failure to heart and learn from them. And remember that a successful business starts with solid fundamental business principles and practices. You will want to continually and systematically put into place processes where you commit, track results, promote accomplishments and get the necessary fuel in the tank to grow your business.[4] Let's start with advice for acquiring a business, since we have advocated from the beginning for this strategy. Then we will work on an exercise to help you start a business.

Buying an Existing Business

If you can't tell already, we wholeheartedly recommend buying an existing business. It can be easier to jump into running a company that has an established clientele paying for the product or service offered. While 82 percent of owners have built their companies from scratch, and a lucky 7 percent inherit their business, we would argue to go with the 11 percent who have purchased their businesses.[5]

To buy a company you will start by hiring a business broker, which you don't have to do, or simply going to websites like Generational Equity, Loopnet, Bizquest.com, and Bizbuysell.

com. Even if you are starting a business from scratch, these websites are good to research existing businesses and how they work. The process of acquiring a business starts similarly to how you would purchase a house or rent an apartment, by looking at these websites, but the back end is obviously different because of the complexities of each business. You can search the available businesses for sale and let the selling broker know if you're interested. They will send you a non-disclosure agreement (NDA), you will sign, and then you will ask for a phone call with the owner. The broker and the seller might check out your LinkedIn page so make sure it is up-to-date and tells your story in the best light possible.

The initial phone call with the seller is one of the best and most interesting parts of the process. It is fascinating to hear them tell their story and learn about their "baby." You can break up questions into the following areas:

- Revenue/Expenses
- Profitability
- Customer Base
- Employee Retention
- Threats
- Growth Opportunities

After the call you will have a conversation with the broker and they will tell you how it went and you can ask more questions. During the entire process you will want to make sure to always go through the business broker and not directly to the seller without the broker's permission. While the seller will have a sell-side broker, as we mentioned before, you aren't required to have a buy-side broker.

You will be able to tell fairly quickly, based on the information you uncover and research about the business, whether you want to move forward. It goes without saying, and might sound simplistic, but it is incredibly important to only move forward with a seller who you feel you can trust. There are just too many variables that they could control to their advantage and you must feel like you can trust them to complete the deal.

If you are interested in moving forward you will submit a letter of intent (LOI) that outlines the price and terms that you would pay for the business. There are templates of LOIs available online and for this step we wouldn't recommend hiring a lawyer (that will come later). In the negotiation about purchase price, we recommend asking for seller equity, or some amount that you pay the seller back over time so it reduces the amount you have to bring to the table. You can usually negotiate up to 30 percent of the total price as a seller note, or seller equity. You might go back and forth on the general idea of the price and terms in the LOI and then ideally you will come to an agreement.

After you come to an agreement, you will need a business lawyer and the seller's broker will ask for your list of items for due diligence. You can find a list online but the items usually fall into the following categories:

- Client Information
- Contracts
- Due Diligence Overview
- Employees
- Financial
- Insurance Coverage
- Market Due Diligence
- New Items
- Organizational Structure
- Operations
- Sales and Marketing
- Taxes

Due diligence usually lasts around two months, and it is important to get all of your questions answered during the process. You can ask your lawyer to help with due diligence and also hire an accounting firm to assist with this step. You will all share a data room, which could be a Dropbox folder, with all of the items that the seller has submitted to you. You will want to set up weekly phone calls with the seller, which the broker will observe. These calls provide a way to develop a rapport with the seller, get direct feedback about the business, and also make sure you reach your goal date for the sale.

During the process of due diligence, you will seek funding. You can get an SBA or conventional loan, privately fund the business, or get the support of friends and family. The funding process is not for the faint of heart. You may be asked to collateralize an existing asset or put forth some equity. You will be asked to turn in a lot of documents to the bank including a personal financial statement, an operating agreement for your new entity with the state, and countless more documents.

If everything checks out, you move forward with a purchase agreement and formally acquire the company. The steps we have described are overly simplified, but they give you a general overview of purchasing an existing company. Don't worry about ever taking yourself too seriously because while any size of a deal will feel enormous to you, during the process your lawyer, banker, accountant, or even close family member will let you know how small your deal is compared to so many others they have either heard about or observed.

Starting a Business: Identify the Pain Point

Now we are going to switch lanes from acquiring a business to starting one of your own. One of the best ways to start a business is to launch something in a field in which you are familiar. Perhaps you have identified a need that you can immediately fill with your existing knowledge and contacts.

If you are struggling to come up with your brilliant idea, let's go through an exercise to help you think of the right business to start. Think very specifically about the pain that made you order this book. When you set up your business you will want to replicate this process of identifying someone's pain and getting them to feel it enough that they'll spend time or money with you (or best of all, both). That pain point will be the basis for your business.

We recommend a few places to start identifying pain points:

1. Identify a point of pain for people in your industry who control a part of the company's budget and create something they could do better, faster or cheaper. Additionally, by sticking to something in your industry, you can use the knowledge and experience you have already gained instead of having to start from scratch.

2. Look at businesses that exist where you could offer something better. While it is tempting to create something new, it is often riskier and costlier. Instead, look at owning a slice of something that is already out there. Remember when choosing a business to run that it is very difficult and costly to change consumer behavior.

3. Talk with family members, friends or people at the coffee shop to ask them about things that would help make their lives easier or better.

4. Survey friends and family members. You could use a website like SurveyMonkey and then compile the data and feedback you get to help you come up with ideas.

5. Join groups around areas that you suspect could produce a pain point. Also, follow certain hashtags and phrases on Twitter using a service like HootSuite to see what people are saying and how they're dealing with a specific pain point.

Some common pain points include:

- Businesses misinforming customers
- Businesses being hard to reach or unresponsive
- Businesses ignoring difficult or confusing aspects of the shopping experience they've created for customers
- Rudeness, on any level of a business
- Unreasonable prices, high delivery fees, or having multiple fees[6]
- Not valuing the customer's support of the business
- Not valuing the customer's time

You may start to see a trend here. Much of running a successful business has to do with being in touch with your customer's needs, expectations, and lifestyle. If you can't connect, provide, and deliver, the customers will go somewhere else. This is why we recommend starting at the point of pain.

When you start with a real problem that you and people you know face, your business ideas won't be fanciful, they'll be practical. For example, take a look at why Amazon has become so successful. It wasn't a proprietary idea to start an online marketplace. What made them stand out was the way they interacted with customers. From providing free shipping and earlier delivery times to Prime members to allowing customers to leave honest reviews, Amazon has communicated to customers that it knows their pain points and has come up with solutions to solve them. Amazon built their reputation as the go-to place for online shopping, based on the customer experience they provide, and their business profited.

Once you have identified the customer pain point you want to target, start coming up with your list of ideas to attend to it. For example, if the pain point you're targeting is that businesses can be hard to reach at times, you might want to build a business around an easy communication service between companies and customers. If you find that people's main complaint is price gouging or high shipping costs, you'll want to make sure that your company addresses that issue by figuring out how to keep costs low.

Choosing your business idea or what business to purchase can seem intimidating. You don't want to waste time on an idea that isn't viable. Now that you have thought about pain points, you can follow these steps to find your big business idea:

1. Brainstorm your ideas to address a pain point or two you've identified. There are some great sites where you can get business ideas, such as on business blogs and websites (entrepreneur.com, *Forbes,* and others).

2. Check out websites of existing businesses such as Generational Equity, Loopnet, Bizquest.com, and Bizbuysell.com to get ideas on good businesses to run.

3. Start eliminating ideas that you think aren't realistic or don't match the type of business you want to create. Prioritize the ones for which you have experience or training.

4. Identify the top ideas where you already have an expertise or connections where you could network to help you achieve your goals.

5. Do some market research. Researching the market for your business is a critical step to determine whether it will succeed.

6. Look at the competition. Is someone already doing your idea? Are they doing it better than what you've come up with so far? If so, you'll need to go back to the drawing board and pick a different pain point, a different market, or come up with a more proprietary solution.

Andre Zafrani, the CEO of Apogee, does management assessments of C-suite executives on behalf of private equity funds and their portfolio companies and Fortune 500 companies. Before launching his business he had a well-developed client base and subject matter proficiency. Zafrani says that running the business from home provides freedom and flexibility without negatively impacting client service and it minimizes operating expenses.

Erin McCarthy and Mindy Turitz started Merinda Studio, which offers artisanal wallpapers, textiles and art inspired by nature. McCarthy says that the two founders have complementary skill sets. Turitz says about working virtually: "We produce our products on demand, which means no inventory management. We can pivot quickly away from a design if it isn't working and ramp up production if something is popular."

David Pikoff, of mobile entertainment company Games2U, said that when they started the business, they knew they wanted it to be mobile and home-based, they never wanted to have a retail business. They created a franchise concept to quickly grow their company and boast more than $3.5 million in sales. They wanted a business that needed very little head count, and one that anybody could own and operate on their own.[7]

Christy Vegosen launched Jewelbox Dress Co., which creates clothing for women with high quality fabrics and modern style. Vegosen says, "I try to use as many local resources as I can, and there are plenty of them right here in Chicago (where we are based). In the fashion industry, word of mouth and a solid reputation will go a long way. Building a trusted circle of people who work ethically and place value on quality is also important."

Why Market Research Matters

When you are creating a business from scratch, market research is important. It allows you to get in touch with consumer behavior and responses, and to make sure that your business idea is grounded in reality. The cost of not doing market research will be that you may be a couple months down the road before you realize that what you're offering isn't what consumers want. You may still have time to pivot, which means changing the course of your business, but you will have used valuable time and resources that could have been channeled toward a more profitable venture.

Market research will be an essential component of your business plan as well. Investors or those you are trying to get a loan from need to be convinced that there's a market for your idea. If you don't have the first-hand testimonies and research to back it up, they'll see it as a pipe dream and move on to the next entrepreneur.

We don't want you to go overboard here, but we do want to give you ideas for making sure your business will thrive. There are two types of market research, and it's good to know both types. This is a good checkpoint to make sure your business idea has a high likelihood to succeed as well as can be proven to someone else. You will want to be sure to communicate these ideas in a sophisticated way.

Conducting Primary Market Research

First, we will start with explaining primary market research. This is the research you will gather first-hand from consumers. You can do this in a number of ways:

- Telephone calls
- Online surveys
- Email surveys
- Pulling from previous sales records if you already have some
- Focus groups

For primary market research, you may develop customer

personas and design a survey to get feedback. A customer persona is basically a statement of your target audience. Think about their age, gender, personality, occupation, lifestyle, geographic location, expendable income, free time, etc.[8] Think about any aspect of them that might have a bearing on making them the perfect consumer for your product or service.

Next, look at the buying habits of your target audience. Where does this type of person usually shop? How much do they spend? What convinces them to make a purchase? What types of features might appeal to them?[9] These are all important questions to ask, to determine how you will go about convincing them to buy from you.

Once you've identified who your customers are and what you think will make them buy from you, it's time to investigate. Make a survey of open-ended questions for potential or past consumers for your business to answer. Open-ended questions will give you the most honest answers and may provide you with information you wouldn't otherwise think to ask for. For example, asking, "What is your least favorite feature of this product?" will lead to more interesting and helpful responses than asking them, "Do you like this product?" or "Would you recommend this product?"

Make sure that the questions you ask get the full picture. This is your chance to hear from your customer, so make sure you take full advantage. Ask them about their background, their job, their lifestyle, and why they would make or have made a purchase from you.[10] You are trying to figure out what variables would need to come together for someone like this person to make a purchase from you.

You can motivate your target audience to take a survey with some kind of incentive, whether that's a free sample of a product or service in the future, a discount, or sending them a thank you gift and note for taking the time to complete it. You can also informally gather customer information. Take a look at the web and you'll see consumer opinions plastered on every page. Whether on Facebook, Twitter, Yelp, Google Reviews, or even the Better Business Bureau, there is a wealth of consumer feedback in your market that is already available. You can add useful information you find here to your growing primary market research findings.

Moving On to Secondary Market Research

Secondary research includes gathering reports, studies, and any relevant information from agencies and trade associations.[11] You will want to research what the market is like for your product or service by comparing it to businesses that are already operating in that space. Some online resources you might want to consider using include:

- *ThomasNet*, a network of industrial businesses and suppliers that provides industry insights.
- *Harris InfoSource All-Industries and Manufacturing Directories*, a tool built to drive sales based on analytics and data.
- *Directory of Associations,* a database to search local, regional, national, or international associations which you can use to gather market statistics and reference materials.
- *The U.S. Census Bureau,* where you can find statistical information for specific counties and areas, business patterns by county, and lists of recent or soon to be released products.
- *USA.gov/business,* information specifically geared towards businesses.
- *Commerce's Economic Indicators* (https://www.commerce. gov/data-and-reports/economic-indicators), which provides censuses and survey feedback concerning the gross domestic product.

- *KnowThis.com* provides mini cases of businesses and market insights from them for a small fee, as well as some free marketing guides.
- *BizMiners.com* provides a selection of reports from the national market from 300 US markets and 16,000 industries for a small fee.
- *MarketResearch.com* contains over 250,000 reports in a regularly updated database. You pay a fee for the sections of the reports that you need.
- *Encyclopedia of Associations*, which includes a list of all associations you can use to find those that relate to your industry.
- *Statistical Abstract of the United States,* which can provide social, economic, and political information pertinent to your business.

Getting connected with associations, local business schools, chamber of commerce, financial and business services can all help with gathering useful information for your marketing research. Most of the information out there is free, but if you don't have time to conduct the research yourself, you can always hire someone to do that part for you.

Use Your Market Research in Your Business Plan

After you have gathered your research, you will compile the data in a way that creates a clear picture. Ultimately, you'll want this to become a part of your business plan. To that end, you want to create a market analysis. Look for any patterns in the market research you conducted.

Consider these questions when you begin writing your market analysis:

- What have your competitors done that worked in the past? Why was it successful?

- What have your competitors done poorly? Why has this cost them?
- What do you plan to do that will give you an edge in this market? Why is it better?
- What results, based on your research, do you think your business efforts will produce?

Why You Should Make a Business Plan ... But Don't Take Too Much Time

You will usually get to choose whether or not to make a business plan. Most of making a business plan depends on your funding sources. In some cases, you won't need any type of formal document or business plan. Just start with an Excel sheet and put in your forecasts. Remember to be honest with yourself about your assumptions and don't be overly optimistic, because that can hurt you later. In other types of businesses and with certain types of funding sources, you will need a business plan. We want to spell out the details of making a business plan but don't want you to focus on it too much, to the detriment of getting started and actually executing.

Making a business plan will do two things for you. One, it will help you to see your business's true potential. The process of writing the business plan is like a simulation. If written out objectively with support from well-done research, it will provide a realistic picture of what your future business will look like and what you can expect. Secondly, it will help you articulate your business plan to future interested parties, including potential investors or future employees.[12] We don't want you to go overboard creating a business plan, but it does help to map out your plans so you are ready and prepared for success.

While writing your business plan, make sure you are being honest about your business and its viability. What may seem like a great idea in your head can begin to tell a different story on paper once you start crunching some numbers. Be willing to table your idea at this point if that different story becomes apparent, and start working on another idea. Your business plan should tell a story of success, but not an overinflated one. An unrealistic business plan won't help you or anyone else who looks at it to make wise decisions about your business.

How to Write Your Business Plan

We're going to walk you through each part of the business plan. To make the process easier for you, you may want to use some of the templates you can find online, such as from the Small Business Administration[13] or from SCORE.[14] The SBA also has some helpful sample business plans.[15]

There are two main types of business plans that are used: a traditional business plan, which is more detailed and often requested by investors, and a lean startup plan, which is a more high-level, focused plan written more for your benefit.[16] If you think you might need an investor at any point, you should probably write the traditional business plan so that you have it on hand when you go looking for money.

When writing your business plan, you may not need to include every section, as some will pertain more to some businesses than others. There is some flexibility in what you include and how you structure it.

For a traditional business plan, you'll want to include:[16]

1. *An Executive Summary* summarizes what your company does and comments on what will lead to its success. This includes a mission statement, information about what your company offers to consumers, and any other pertinent information about your company such as its structure, leadership, geographic location, and industry. If you are planning to ask for funding, you'll want to talk about your plan for growth here, too, so that an

investor can have some assurance from the first section that they'll get a return on their investment.

2. *A Company Description* provides information about the pain point your business is addressing and what its solution is to that problem. You'll want to include the target audience you came up with for your marketing research to show who your company aims to reach. Include what makes your business different from others in its industry and will give you a competitive edge.

3. *Market Analysis* shows that there's a good market for what you're doing and why your company is poised to reach your intended market.

4. *Organization and Management* identifies the leadership and structure of your company in more detail. Including a visual chart of the structure can be informative for you and your teammates and help you when you need to communicate it to investors. You'll want to mention what type of corporation you are (C, S, LLC), and resumes or CVs from key players on your team.

5. *Service or Product Line* describes what your company offers, whether a product or service, and tells what intellectual property rights you have bought or plan to buy. You can detail any future research and development you plan to do in this area here, too.

6. *Marketing and Sales* shows the strategy you've come up with to continually grow your sales. You'll also show how a sale will take place.

7. *Funding Request* for an investor or lender. Here you'll detail your financial needs, the period of time you'll need it for, specifics about what you'll use it for, whether you want to use debt or equity, and a plan to pay it back.

8. *Financial Projections* can be a continuation of your funding request. The aim of this section is to show that your business will be financially stable in the future.

You'll want to provide a financial forecast of the next five years, including income, balance, cash flow, and capital expenses. The first year should show monthly projections. Use graphs and charts to explain this section as clearly as possible.

9. *Appendix* is a place to put any other documents that might have a bearing on your business or that are requested by a lender or investor. This might include your resume, credit history, references, patents, permits, legal documents, contracts, etc.

If you aren't planning on talking to investors or lenders and you are creating a business plan for your own purposes, you might want to write a lean startup plan that includes more basic elements. If you are short on time, it can also be helpful to start with the lean business plan and then write out the more traditional plan a little further down the road. The bottom line is, whichever plan you choose, a business plan will act as your guide and help you articulate key points about your business.

You'll want to include the following in your lean startup plan, taken from the Business Model Canvas (free template: https://miro.com/templates/business-model-canvas/):

1. *Key Partnerships* introduce other businesses or parties you plan to work with, including manufacturers and suppliers.
2. *Key Activities* list the activities your business will do to give it a competitive edge.
3. *Key Resources* list what you have that add value to your product or service, including intellectual property rights, your team, capital, etc.
4. *Value Proposition* shows the unique value your business offers in comparison to competitors.
5. *Customer Relationships* relates the customer experience,

from the first contact to their final experience.

6. *Customer Segments* discuss your target market(s).

7. *Channels* show how you'll reach and communicate with your customers.

8. *Cost Structure* list the costs of marketing and product development you anticipate and how your company will offset those.

9. *Revenue Streams* show how your company will produce revenue. List any sales, membership fees, subscription fees, or any other kind of income.

What to Do Before You Financially Commit to Your Business

After writing your business plan, and seeing how your dreams are going to come true, you are probably eager to rush to the next step. In the next chapter, we'll show you how to network effectively to set you up for success and how to get the funding you need using the business plan you just created. Before you move ahead, we wanted to share with you some things you will need to know before you financially commit to this venture.

New businesses can fail, and quickly. Your first idea might not pan out. With that in mind, weigh your risks carefully and take the planning process seriously. If your business does fail, learn from your mistakes. Then, the next time you can be ready. The good news is that more small businesses than ever are making it past the first year, as we mentioned before, with only 22.5% of them failing.[17]

Only make hires on an as-needed basis while your company is getting off the ground. In the small business world, over 60% of home-based businesses haven't hired staff. Making hires can be costly, both in time and money. Don't offer your best friend's son a job just yet, unless he's a genius in your area of business.

Small businesses are more often in debt than not, with as much as 68% of them being in debt at any given time. Approximately

67% of small business owners also end up having to use their personal funds to help their business. If you're doing the math, you'll see that there's an overlap of small business owners who are in debt and using their own funds at the same time to help their business survive. Make sure that your spouse and family are on board with these financial risks before you move forward, or plan so that you aren't in a position where you'll need to pour everything you have into your business to the extent that you risk bankruptcy. One way to do this is to create an emergency fund specifically for your business, so that you don't end up putting your personal financial well-being on the line.

It also may take longer to get your business going than you expect. Some entrepreneurs spend three or more years in the grind, working hard until they start to see some growth.[18] You will need to be resilient, diligent, and press on. Remember the start of this chapter? Go forward with cautious optimism and excitement for the ability and chance to start out on your own as a CEO from home.

Chapter 3 Key Takeaways
After reading this chapter, what should you understand?

1. Harness cautious optimism when starting your business.
2. Learn how to acquire a business and alternatively get tips on coming up with your business idea.
3. Identify a pain point that you want to solve and roadblocks to getting started.
4. Try to start a business in an industry that you know.

Endnotes

1   Dragomir Simovic. "39 Entrepreneur Statistics You Need to Know in 2020." Accessed October 7, 2020. https://www.smallbizgenius.net/by-the-numbers/entrepreneur-statistics/#gref

2   Patrick Henry. "Why Some Startups Succeed (And Why Most Fail)." Accessed October 7, 2020. https://www. entrepreneur.com/article/288769

3   Dragomir Simovic. "39 Entrepreneur Statistics You Need to Know in 2020." Accessed October 7, 2020. https:// www.smallbizgenius.net/by-the-numbers/entrepreneur-statistics/#gref

4   Patrick Henry. "Why Some Startups Succeed (And Why Most Fail)." Accessed October 7, 2020. https://www. entrepreneur.com/article/288769

5   Dragomir Simovic. "39 Entrepreneur Statistics You Need to Know in 2020." Accessed October 7, 2020. https:// www.smallbizgenius.net/by-the-numbers/entrepreneur-statistics/#gref

6   Rob Starr. "7 Most Common Customer Pain Points and How to Fix Them." Accessed May 14, 2020. https://smallbiztrends. com/2018/06/most-common-customer-pain-points.html

7   Tamara Schweitzer. "How to Run a Business From Home." Accessed October 7, 2020. https://www.inc.com/ss/how-run-business-home

8   "The Best Ways to Do Market Research for Your Business Plan." Accessed May 14, 2020. https://www.entrepreneur. com/article/241080

9   "The Best Ways to Do Market Research for Your Business Plan." Accessed May 14, 2020. https://www.entrepreneur. com/article/241080

10 Debbie Farese. "How to Do Market Research: A 6-Step Guide." Accessed May 14, 2020. https://blog.hubspot.com/ marketing/market-research-buyers-journey-guide

11 "Conducting Market Research." Accessed May 14, 2020. https://www.entrepreneur.com/article/217388

12 Jeff Haden. "How to Write the Perfect Business Plan: A Comprehensive Guide." Accessed May 14, 2020. https:// www.inc.com/jeff-haden/how-to-write-perfect-business-

plan-a-comprehensive-guide.html

13 Business Plan Template. Accessed July 8, 2020. https://www.sba.gov/business-guide/plan-your-business/write-your-business-plan

14 Business Plan Template. Accessed July 8, 2020. https://www.score.org/resource/business-plan-template-startup-business

15 Business Plan Template. Accessed July 8, 2020. https://www.bplans.com/sbp/sample_business_plans.php

16 "Write Your Business Plan." Accessed May 14, 2020. https://www.sba.gov/business-guide/plan-your-business/write-your-business-plan

17 Dragomir Simovic. "39 Entrepreneur Statistics You Need to Know in 2020." Accessed May 15, 2020. https://www.smallbizgenius.net/by-the-numbers/entrepreneur-statistics/#gref

18 Mandela SH Dixon. "6 Things No One Tells You (But Really Should) About Starting a Company." Accessed May 15, 2020. https://medium.com/@MandelaSH/6-things-no-one-tells-you-but-really-should-about-starting-a-company-f17574a88378

Chapter 4

Fund Your Idea

You are now armed with a chosen CEO type, industry, and ideas ready for a business. Next up, it is time to talk about money. One of the biggest issues you can face is a lack of funding, or being too ambitious and trying to do too much too soon. This chapter is action-packed with every detail you could want or need on how to fund your new business.

We will spend time talking about funding businesses that you acquire versus businesses that you start on your own. There are some similarities and a few differences. If you buy a business, you will have more parameters around the amount of money required and the overall financial expectations of the business. You will also most likely earn some type of salary from the beginning.

In terms of starting a business from scratch, some don't require a lot of capital to get off the ground while others require a lot. Depending on your situation, you might need to continue working as you were before, but do so more strategically. You may need the stability your job provides while you test your ideas and get funding and support. On the other hand, you might have developed a runway of time and money to help yourself get your business off the ground. This chapter will move through all of your options.

Assess Your Financial Needs

Before you can figure out how to fund your business, you need to assess your financial needs. In the previous chapter we talked about making your business plan. You will find that one of the most important sections of that plan is the financial section. If you are playing by all the rules and putting a business plan together with a specific financial section, when you approach a potential backer or investor they will want to see if your business is financially viable.

Whether you have a financial plan or a simple sheet that shows your financing needs, it should serve to answer any possible questions an investor might have about your finances. You will also want to prepare financial projections in terms of the worst- and best-case scenarios, so that your investors can see the range of risk and potential profit your business has to offer.

The financial section should include:

- Income statement (expenses, revenues, profits)
- Anticipated cash flow
- Balance sheet
- Profit and loss statement[1]

Ideally, the financial section of your business plan should cover monthly projections (cash revenue projections) for the first year and quarterly information for the next two years. This will help you calculate your gross margin.[2] You will also want to include an accounting of cash disbursements, or expenditures, for each month. To get the cash flow balance that will be carried over to the next month, simply subtract the disbursements from the revenue.

In your balance sheet, you will need to show the total worth of your business, or owner's equity. You will list your assets, liabilities, and balance. Then, you will want to include a breakeven analysis. This is where you show the timeline for your sales to catch up with the expenses. Lastly, if your business has had historical operations, it might be wise to include a business financial history section to instill confidence. You want these numbers to reflect the potential for your business to produce profit, as well as a realistic amount of money you will need as you start your business. If you're not great with numbers, you will want to work with someone who is, or use some financial planning software. Don't get intimidated by the process, as in some cases it can be very casual. But take our advice to heart and be mindful about your financial planning.

Funding an Acquired Business

When you are evaluating a business to acquire you are undoubtedly spending a lot of time with its numbers. Specifically, you want to look through the company's profit and loss statements and balance sheets to verify that its existing EBITDA (earnings before interest, taxes, depreciation, and amortization) will support your debt service, your salary and any improvements that you want to make to the business. Your purchase price will be based on a multiple of that EBITDA, and more specifically the seller's discretionary earnings, or SDE.

You have a few options for paying for the business once you have established an overall purchase price. You can ask the seller for a seller note, which means that you will pay back a portion of the overall purchase price, which is usually some number up to 30 percent. You pay this back over time, which is usually a period of three to five years. You will need to come up with the other 70 percent. You might have the money ready to go or have very generous friends and family who are willing to invest. You could provide the seller with an earn-out as part of the structure. You can also ask the business broker or your own banker for leads on an SBA lender. They will ask for your personal financial statement and most likely check through a quick business plan and some references and then might extend you financing for the business. We will provide more details on SBA funding and other routes of funding as we go through the options to fund a business that you start.

Funding a Business You Start

Depending on what type of CEO and business that you are

pursuing there will be different solutions to funding a business that you start. You might be a gig owner CEO, which lends itself to starting something while you are working as an independent contractor and can be fairly straightforward. You might be a traditional owner CEO and acquire a business. Or, regardless of which CEO from home that you decide to be, you might not have to invest a lot and can jump right in. But for now, we are going to focus our advice on the active traditional owner CEO who is starting something from scratch with a larger investment necessary. It may not sound appealing to do two things at once, but it might be necessary in the beginning stages of your business to continue your work while starting your business. Ideally you will be working in the same industry as the business you are starting. If you are switching to a different industry, you may need to change your job to something that will give you experience as you are starting your business. The key during this transitional time is to keep yourself afloat financially while building your at-home business. If you can afford it, you may want to consider transferring to a part-time job so you have the necessary time and energy to get your business off the ground.

Networking to Raise Money for Your Business

Building a business network used to mean working the room at a conference or trade show, meeting as many people as possible and trading business cards. This can still lead to some meaningful business partnerships, but the digital world has of course added a whole new element to networking. Especially in a post-COVID world, people are meeting and developing business relationships without ever having met or spoken on the phone.

If you are working from home and trying to build your startup, chances are it will be a more effective means of networking if you can connect with others online. You can use some social media for this purpose, or you can try some websites and applications that were specifically designed for this.

It's always wise to start with your current network. Ask friends and family on social media to help you spread the word about your business and any investment opportunities. For example, if you created a Facebook business page and invited twenty friends, they could re-post and comment on your content, which would then appear on the feeds of all their Facebook friends who follow them. Word of mouth can travel online sometimes faster and more effectively than in-person. This could be an important asset, as each of those people you are connected to are connected to many other people you wouldn't normally be able to reach.

When you are starting out, you need to build your network to spread awareness of your business and brand, but you also need to network if you need help with funding the business. LinkedIn is the largest of these and we would highly recommend seeking out connections here. Other business networking sites you might want to check out include:

- **100AM networking.**[3] Designed with a unique event networking flow, 100AM networking allows you to schedule meetings or chat one on one with someone planning on attending an event, allows you to scan business cards, and allows you to add contacts from the event to your address book.
- **Networking for Professionals.** Networking for Professionals combines traditional networking through events, with the addition of an online platform. They also have advertisements on their website and in their newsletter your business could be featured in!
- **E-Factor.** E-Factor enables affiliates to collaborate with partners and clients in a virtual marketplace as well as in-person. This platform makes you visible to potential business partners and gives you information on others on

the platform.

- **Gust**. Geared towards startups. Gust helps connect them with a range of investors across the globe. You can apply to be added to investment groups and investors can review your information, contact you via messenger, and notify you if they are interested in investing.
- **Opportunity**. This business network is based on referrals. It connects you with businesses that can refer you to others and others to you. They've also added in-person events to even stronger connections.
- **Ryze**. This platform has features such as messenger, groups, and practical articles to help you connect with other businesses. Ryze also provides the ability to make deals with other businesses.
- **StartupNation**. As an online forum for business startups, here you have the ability to ask questions to gain business knowledge and insight. There are articles you can glean tips from and you can connect with other professionals for future networking purposes.
- **BNI**. This organization helps with business referrals. They aim to help their members make quality business connections.
- **Shapr**. This platform connects people with the same types of businesses and interests.
- **Eventbrite**. Though not specifically designed for business, Eventbrite hosts virtual events for business networking which could prove fruitful for your business.

Now that you have some ideas for where to network online, I'm sure you're wondering how to do it. Do you simply strike up a conversation with someone who has a similar business to yours? Should you go straight into pitching them an idea for a business collaboration?

The Dos:

- Regularly update your bios and profile pictures on business networking sites
- Share helpful articles and business tips with other business professionals
- Contribute to publications in your industry
- Make a holiday E-card mailing list
- Post updates about your business (new hires, projects, successes)
- Write a personal note to those you've met at events or through others saying you want to connect on the business platform
- Create an email signature listing your business and contact information[4]
- Congratulate others on their business success
- Offer to help others get connected with other businesses
- Target your top 20 people to connect meaningful with in the business world, then 50 you want to connect with on a more social level ("smart networking")
- Find a way to help someone you want to connect with ... remember to give first
- Form connections with promising individuals early in their career[5]

The Don'ts:

- Try to connect with as many people as possible ("random networking")[6]
- Sign up to be on more online platforms than you can handle
- Continue talking to someone about your business who doesn't seem interested
- Inundate those others with too much information and

don't contact them too often
- Lose contact with your most meaningful business contacts
- Continually send potential investors or business contacts new ideas for projects and businesses

Crowdfunding

In addition to networking you can pursue crowdfunding. This type of funding includes kickstarter campaigns and Gofundme pages. Crowdfunding is when an individual or business gathers individual investors to fund their project, whether that is a startup or a new project for a current business. The websites designed for crowdfunding require a screening process and charge a fee, but they will also bring a lot of publicity to your business venture. Some crowdfunding statistics you may want to think about are:[7]

- Successful crowdfunding campaigns bring in $7,000 on average.
- Most crowdfunding campaigns last nine weeks.
- The most successful crowdfunding campaigns meet 30% of their goal in the first week.

There are four main types of crowdfunding:[8]

- Reward crowdfunding. With reward crowdfunding, you give those who make a financial donation some type of reward or incentive, such as a free product sample, prototype, or something with your company's logo on it. You can incentivize investors by giving better rewards to people who give more. The catch is, you have to offer something people actually want or could use.
- Donation crowdfunding. Donation crowdfunding is as it sounds. People make donations without expecting anything in return. This can be harder to convince people

to do unless they already have a personal connection with you and your business.

- Equity crowdfunding. Equity crowdfunding is a little more complicated. You give your financial backers a small share of your business. You have to be careful with this one, as you don't want to give too much of your business away. There are also some important laws and regulations you will need to abide by. Do your research if you want to go this route.
- Debt crowdfunding. This type of crowdfunding means the funding your backers provide will need to be repaid, with interest, and within a pre-designated amount of times, usually no more than five years. You must have good credit to be eligible for this.

You should consider crowdfunding if your business wants to create a new product or is doing a trial run of a product. It's also ideal if you are already active on social media and have a network that would fund you, as you will need to maintain an active online campaign. Crowdfunding doesn't work so well when you need long-term funding for your business. Also, if you need a sizeable investment of over five figures you should look at other options. Crowdfunding isn't ideal if you have a credit history that is non-existent or bad.

There is increasing competition among crowdfunding companies. This helps keep the cost of these campaigns low and is one of the reasons they have become so popular. Each of these crowdfunding platforms, in addition to charging a fee for using their platform, charges a processing fee. Even so, on average you will walk away from a successful campaign with more than 90% of the funding you raise.

Crowdfunding platforms to consider:

- *Kickstarter.* This is a reward crowdfunding site, which means it is best for businesses that have something tangible they can offer their backers as a reward. Think about businesses that produce clothing, electronic gear, sports or hobby equipment, and the like. They charge a competitive 5% fee.
- *Indiegogo.* Another reward crowdfunding site, Indiegogo is similarly structured to suit businesses with something tangible to offer backers. They also charge a 5% fee for successfully funded campaigns.
- *GoFundMe.* As a donation crowdfunding site, GoFundMe has an appeal. Backers merely donate funds because they believe in your business or project and want to support you, no strings attached. There is no fee for the campaign, but there is a small transaction fee. Before you decide on this option, you may want to consider whether people will actually be motivated to give to your business without getting anything in return.
- *Fundly.* Another donation crowdfunding site, Fundly is unique in that you don't have to meet your goal in the allotted amount to walk away with the cash. They charge a 4.9% fee along with processing fees.
- *Crowdfunder.* This site offers a form of equity crowdfunding. You pay a monthly subscription of $499 or less and are offered access to investors who may be interested in backing your business. The platform helps with customer relationship management (CRM), too. You may want to use this platform if you are looking to raise a more substantial amount of money and have more control over investor selection.
- *WeFunder.* Another equity crowdfunding site, WeFunder is used by business in technology, entertainment, restaurants, and many other fields. Many people who use this site already have an established network of backers

and merely use it as a platform to facilitate transactions, as well as to attract some new interest. You may want to use this if you already have an established network, as they have a single fee of 7.5%. However, this may not be the best option for startups that do not yet have an established network.

- *LendingClub*. A debt crowdfunding site, LendingClub will allow you to fundraise up to $300,000 (depending on your credit), which must be repaid within five years or less. Their interest rates start at 5.99% annually. There are certain credit and revenue requirements you and your business must meet to use this platform. This is a good option if you need access to the funds quickly, as you can get that within about a week of starting.
- *Prosper*. Another debt crowdfunding site is Prosper, where you can get a loan of up to $40,000. The credit and revenue requirements to use this platform are a little more relaxed than LendingClub. This platform will provide you with the cash you need quickly, but after receiving the loan you'll need to begin monthly payments with a total APR ranging from 7.5% up to 41%.

Tips for successful crowdfunding:

1. Tell your company's story in a compelling way
2. Use great visuals
3. Advertise to the network you already have (friends, family, business connections)
4. Connect with your target audience
5. Make a realistic funding goal
6. Keep your backers updated and reassure them in their investment
7. Maintain a strong social media presence
8. Be your own PR team and don't expect the platform to

do all the work for you

Angel Investor

An angel investor is a person with a large amount of money to invest in a promising startup company. They usually don't have to be paid back if your startup fails, but as they are usually business professionals themselves, they're going to be savvy enough to not invest in a bad business plan.

Because of their experience, angel investors can add a lot of value to your startup. However, they aren't making a charitable donation. They are purchasing a stake in your company, and unless they want to be a silent partner you will need to consider how their input will affect your business.[9] In terms of finding an angel investor, you can use the network you have begun to build to get connected. You can also look through the Angel Capital Association (https://www.angelcapitalassociation.org/), where you will find a list of investors and more information about this type of funding.

After you connect with an angel investor, you need to be respectful of their time and succinctly tell them what your business is about and why you need their funding. Additionally, they will want to see that you know your stuff. You can impress them with your business plan and your well-researched financial projections. Sell them on your passion and personal investment in the project.

There is a chance that you might strike out with your angel investor. It's wise to keep the angel investor appraised of how your business is doing with the chance that they might want to invest further down the line.[10] On the flip side, if your angel says yes make sure that you are clear about the equity stake the angel has in the company and how much input they will or won't be able to contribute.

Venture Capital

Venture capital (VC) comes from a venture capital firm. The individuals from these firms, venture capitalists, invest money from their firm's fund in startups that have great potential.

Just like with the angel investor, you can use some of the networking sites to find a venture capitalist who might be interested in helping you get your startup off the ground. Once you have connected with a potential venture capital investor and they have confirmed that their firm is interested, you will want to share your business plan with them. Make sure that when you decide to do business with them, the terms of your agreement are detailed and thorough.

The US Small Business Administration advises before partnering with a venture capitalist that you do background research to make sure it is a reputable firm.[11] Venture capital is not the best funding option for everyone. You may want to go this route if:

- You are a fast-growing startup that needs a lot of capital and possibly some direction from seasoned professionals
- You would rather part with equity than accrue debt
- You want a financing partner who is in it for the long haul, not just the startup stage[12]

You can check out various venture capital firms at tech market intelligence platforms such as CBinsights (https://www.cbinsights.com/). You can also find venture capital through Fintech companies such as Pitchbook.

Pledge Future Earnings

Another possible means of funding, if you don't want to give away equity and you are not fond of the idea of accruing debt, is to pledge your future earnings in exchange for capital up front. This is a type of venture capital, but with a non-traditional structure. This structure ensures that, if your business should fail, the investor would lose out as well, so you will have to make a convincing case that your business will become very profitable in the near future.

You will need to attract investors through networking, similar to finding angel investors and venture capital. You will show them your savvy business plan with a clear, promising financial future mapped out. Then, you can use an online marketplace such as the Thrust Fund to offer a percentage of your future earnings in exchange for funding.[13]

Family and Friends as Investors

Another possible way you could finance your startup is with the support of family and friends. In fact, more than 70% of all capital for startups comes from family and friends.[14]

Even though you already have an established relationship with your family and friends, you should still show them your formal business plan and financial projections. Don't make the mistake of thinking that they will be understanding if you can't pay them back on time or at all if your business fails.

Make sure your friend or family member knows the risks involved in supporting your business. Put the terms of your agreement in writing so that there is clarity about how and when they will be paid back, as well as whether there will be any interest or equity involved.[15] The important thing to remember is to approach and treat your family member or friend with the same level of respect and financial responsibility you would give to an angel investor or venture capitalist.

Bank Loans

Loans play a large part in small businesses, as 59 percent of entrepreneurs who apply for a loan use it to expand their business.[16] You may want to consider taking out a bank loan if:

- You need a substantial amount of cash
- You have a healthy, realistic financial plan for your business
- You have a great credit score
- You have something you can use as collateral

Taking out a bank loan for your at-home business startup has some administrative hoops but can be done. Here are the steps involved:[17]

1. Check your credit
2. Decide on your method of incorporation (LLC, C, S) and file paperwork with your state
3. Make sure you have a sound financial plan for your business
4. Figure out the classification of your business according to the NAICS code
5. Apply for a loan, which can take 2–3 months. You may want to apply for several loans at the same time. When applying you will do the following:
   - Explain your revenue, customer base, and method of sales
   - Decide if you have something you can provide as collateral to help your case
   - Discuss fees, payments and particulars with your lender before application submission
   - Bring all potentially relevant documentation to meet with a banker about your loan application, which may include your personal or business credit report or tax returns, your business plan, balance sheets, and even your resume

SBA Loans

SBA loans are regulated by the Small Business Administration and are in high demand for small businesses. An SBA loan is a popular option for a lot of small businesses. To get this type of loan, you will need to apply with a financial company that processes SBA loans. These financial companies may have additional restrictions.[18]

According to the SBA, there are various types of programs for different types of businesses.

- The Small Business Investment Companies (SBIC) are private. They use a combination of their own funds and those borrowed from the SBA. They make both equity and debt investments.
- The Small Business Innovation Research (SBIR) program supports small businesses doing federal research and development that could be commercialized.
- The Small Business Technology Transfer (STTR) program gives funding to businesses that are doing federal research and development. These businesses usually work with nonprofit institutions as a startup.[19]

Types of Loans:[20]

7(a) loan program

- These can be used for a variety of purposes: buying machinery or equipment or furniture, purchasing real estate, leasehold improvements, working capital or even debt refinancing
- 10–25 years for loan maturation
- Includes express programs (available quickly), export loan programs (for companies that export), rural lender advantage program, and special purpose loans program
- Capped at potentially $2 million through lender

CDC/504 loan program

- Long-term, fixed rate loan
- Usually to buy real estate, equipment, or means to expand

Steps to take:

1. Through your network or research, connect with an SBA lender
2. Submit the necessary documents to the SBA lender
3. If successful, you will receive a term sheet for the financing

SBA Microloans

If you don't have a credit history or collateral and you only need a small loan ($35,000 or less), you might want to consider a microloan. The SBA has a microloan program, providing short-term loans for up to $35,000. These can be used on a number of business-related expenses, such as purchasing inventory, needed supplies or equipment.

To get a microloan, you need to find a microlender, which is usually a nonprofit. Microloans are smaller but more flexible and there are fewer hoops to jump through to qualify. The downside is that some of the lenders charge slightly higher interest rates than a bank would charge.

Reasons to get a microloan:

1. You can borrow money in small amounts so that you don't take out a bigger loan than you need
2. SBA microloans have a simple structure with equal monthly payments
3. Microlenders want your business to succeed and are often willing to help you with the planning process

4. If you don't have much credit history, you can take out a small loan to build credit first

Steps to take:

1. Fill out the application
2. Supply your microlender with:
   - Your government ID
   - Proof of cash flow
   - Financial statements and documents
   - A detailed list of what the loan will be used for
   - Your business plan
   - How you have personally invested in the business
   - Possible collateral
   - References
3. The loan officer may come to your home office and assess anything you want to use as collateral
4. Upon approval, your loan may be deposited directly into your bank account. Remember not to have it deposited in your personal bank account, to keep accounting separate
5. After disbursement, your payment plan will begin as agreed upon. If you ever have trouble paying, reach out to your lender

Credit Cards

While credit card debt is notorious for getting out of hand, if you are able to manage it well, it could help your home business startup. One tip to keep you out of trouble: don't mix your personal and business expenses. Get a credit card exclusively for your business.

In fact, there are places that are happy to provide you with a business credit card, such as retailers like Costco or Staples. These usually come with special business discounts or coupons. Additionally, if you are just starting out and haven't built up your credit score yet, getting a business credit card, using it and paying it off quickly can give your score a boost, enabling you to pursue future funding.[21]

Factoring

In factoring, instead of waiting for your customers to pay to put that cash back into the business, you "sell" the invoices of your customers to a factor. This factor will usually pay you 85–95 percent of the payment up front so that you don't have to wait to receive it from the customer. The factor then waits for the customer to pay them. They will give you the remaining 5–15% after the customer pays them, deducting a fee. These fees will probably add up to 1 to 6 percent of your total invoice value each month out of those you have sold for factoring. As you can see, this method is a faster way to get cash up front.[22]

Factoring also has the potential to turn into a long business relationship, if invoices continue to be purchased by a company. This way of raising capital is not used as often in the United States as it is in other countries. Only a couple of banks, including Wells Fargo and CIT, are big competitors in this area.[23]

Here are a couple companies you might want to consider looking at if you are considering financing through factoring:

Breakout Capital
- Receive up to $500,000
- Up to 24 months repayment term
- Fees start at 1.25% per month
- No revenue, credit score, or time in business requirements

Fundbox
- Receive up to $100,000
- 12–24 months repayment term
- Advance fees start at 4.66%
- Must be US-based business, sync your accounting

software to Fundbox, and have a credit score of 500+ to qualify

Lendio
- Finance aggregator that connects you to 75+ top US financers
- Has other financial options such as short-term loans, SBA loans, and equipment financing.
- It's advisable to have a credit score of 550+ and to have been in business for 3+ months

P2BInvestor
- Receive $250,000 to $10 million in asset-backed lines of credit
- 1-year revolving terms
- Fees start at 17%
- Lines of credit are secured using accounts receivables and/or inventory
- Must have annual revenue of $500,000 and been in business 6+ months

Riviera Finance
- Receive up to $2 million for unpaid invoices
- 6 month contract
- Rates start at 2%
- No revenue, credit score, or time in business requirements

Provide Your Own Funding
If you don't want to worry about having to repay loans or share your business decisions or profit with anyone else, you may want to consider self-funding your business. Many people decide to use their own funding, whether it's their life savings, the money they have put away for their child's college education, or their emergency fund. Self-funding comes with its own risks,

however, such as sinking your savings into a business that fails, with no way to get back the money.

The internal revenue code allows individuals to use their 401K to invest in an operating company, but the company must be selling or exchanging products or services.[24] If used correctly, this can turn into a profitable endeavor, and one that can be folded into a new 401K. You may want to consider the risks, however, if you're thinking of using your retirement funds or 401K to fund your business. You should ensure you do everything by the book, or else you risk getting saddled with hefty penalty fees. There are companies that can help you navigate these murky waters, such as Guidant Financial (https://www.guidantfinancial.com/financing-solutions/401k-business-financing/).

Chapter 4 Key Takeaways
After reading this chapter, what should you understand?

1. When purchasing a business you will evaluate its existing cash flow to ensure that it will support your debt service, your salary and any necessary improvements.
2. Make a thorough financial section of your business plan.
3. Network to make meaningful business connections.
4. Beware of money traps like expensive web development and legal fees.
5. Consider your funding options carefully:
   - Crowdfunding
   - Angel Investors
   - Venture Capital
   - Promising Future Funds
   - Family and Friends
   - Factoring
   - Loans
   - Credit Cards

- Factoring
- Self-Funding

Endnotes

1   Sonal Mishra. "How to write a financial section for your Startup Business Plan?" Accessed April 18, 2020. https://up-metrics.co/blog/write-financial-section-startup-business-plan

2   Elizabeth Wasserman. "How to Write the Financial Section of a Business Plan." Accessed April 18, 2020. https://www.inc.com/guides/business-plan-financial-section.html

3   "10 Best Business Networking Sites." Accessed April 16, 2020. https://blog.100am.co/10-best-business-networking-sites/

4   Kelly Hoey. "20 Ways to Build A Strong Business Network – Without Leaving Your Desk." Accessed April 16, 2020. https://www.forbes.com/sites/kellyhoey/2018/08/22/20-ways-to-build-a-strong-business-network-without-leaving-your-desk/#5bfa18093ac7

5   Minda Zetlin. "How to Network Like You Really Mean It." Accessed April 16, 2020. https://www.inc.com/minda-zetlin/8-things-power-networkers-do-make-connections.html

6   "Marketing & Sales: Schmoozing Your Way to Business Success." Accessed April 16, 2020. https://www.entrepreneur.com/article/65692

7   "Key Crowdfunding Statistics." Accessed April 17, 2020. https://www.startups.com/library/expert-advice/key-crowdfunding-statistics

8   Tricia Tetreault. "How to Crowdfund Your Small Business." Accessed April 16, 2020. https://fitsmallbusiness.com/how-to-crowdfund-small-business/

9   The Startup Team. "Angel Investors Vs. Venture Capitalists." By The Startup Team. Accessed April 18, 2020. https://

www.startups.com/library/expert-advice/angel-investors-vs-venture-capitalists

10 Kasey Wehrum. "Get Your Wings." Accessed April 16, 2020. https://www.inc.com/magazine/20090101/get-your-wings.html

11 US Small Business Administration. "Fund Your Business." Accessed April 16, 2020. https://www.sba.gov/business-guide/plan-your-business/fund-your-business

12 US Small Business Administration. "Fund Your Business." Accessed April 16, 2020. https://www.sba.gov/business-guide/plan-your-business/fund-your-business

13 Inc Staff. "10 Ways to Finance Your Business." Accessed April 16, 2020. https://www.inc.com/guides/2010/07/how-to-finance-your-business.html

14 Alison Stein Wellner. "Blood Money." Accessed April 16, 2020. https://www.inc.com/magazine/20031201/gettingstarted.html

15 Inc Staff. "10 Ways to Finance Your Business." Accessed April 16, 2020. https://www.inc.com/guides/2010/07/how-to-finance-your-business.html

16 https://www.smallbizgenius.net/by-the-numbers/entrepreneur-statistics/#gref

17 Christine Lagorio-Chafkin. "How to Fill Out a Loan Application." Accessed April 16, 2020. https://www.inc.com/guides/filling-out-loan-application.html

18 Inc Staff. "10 Ways to Finance Your Business." Accessed April 16, 2020. https://www.inc.com/guides/2010/07/how-to-finance-your-business.html

19 US Small Business Administration. "Fund Your Business." Accessed April 16, 2020. https://www.sba.gov/business-guide/plan-your-business/fund-your-business

20 Inc Staff. "How to Secure an SBA Loan." April 16, 2020. https://www.inc.com/guides/2010/04/securing-sba-loan.html

21 Bobbie Gossage. "Charging Ahead." Accessed April 16,

2020. https://www.inc.com/magazine/20040101/gettingstar ted.html

22 Erica Seppala. "Best Factoring Companies for Small Business." Accessed April 20, 2020. https://www.merchantmaverick.com/best-factoring-companies/

23 Hannah Clark Steiman. "Short on Cash?" Accessed April 16, 2020. https://www.inc.com/magazine/20080101/short-on-cash.html

24 Matt Quinn. "How to Finance a Business with Your 401(k)." Accessed April 16, 2020. https://www.inc.com/guides/2010/05/financing-a-business-with-your-401k.html

Chapter 5

Get Feedback

Even though you will be leading from home doesn't mean you want to go it alone. You are going to need feedback from the beginning. If you are a residual owner CEO you will need mentor relationships to help with your investments and projects. A gig owner CEO might need a mentor or small informal board to help kick off their business. A traditional owner CEO might need to test their product or service and develop mentors and potentially a board of directors. Just like they say about raising children, running a business requires a village.

Feedback is essential because you don't want to waste time reinventing the wheel. For almost all of the decisions you will make, whether they be starting a website, investing in a commercial property, launching a new product, or acquiring a company, someone has gone before you. Even if you are starting a company from scratch, others have done this too. While for some it is hard and humbling to reach out, more than anything it saves you valuable time and resources. We urge you, regardless of what type of CEO from home you wish to be, to seek support and ask for feedback.

Mentorship is critical for the CEO from home. A mentor is in your corner rooting for you to win and helping to point out potential obstacles along the way. Developing a solid mentor relationship can in some cases mean the difference between your company thriving or failing. For the greatest success in this area, try to find a CEO that is the same type that you were, or had previous experience as that type.

Where Do You Find a Good Mentor?
A mentor can be anywhere. A mentor could be a long-time

friend, a friend's parent, a former professor or teacher, a business acquaintance, or a former boss. You might have an informal relationship or a formal one where you meet quarterly or annually. In most cases, it does well to recognize the person as the mentor that they are and thank them for the help they provide to you.

If you need help finding a mentor, we suggest starting with your contacts and LinkedIn. It will take some hustle to find a good one. If you can't find a mentor who is a good fit through networking, there are many resources out there for connecting with experts in your field:

- Small Business Development Centers (SBDCs) can connect you with experts, provide resources, and provide invaluable advice for your industry. You can get a free consultation from SBDCs as they are federally and locally funded by the Small Business Administration.
- SCORE will connect you with a mentor who is available at specific times of the week. You can receive real-time mentoring through this organization. Since they are a nonprofit partner of the Small Business Administration, they provide free mentoring services. Additionally, you can visit a mentor as many times as you like. They have more than 11,000 volunteer mentors in their program, in many different fields.
- Industry Expos and Conferences can be a way to find a mentor in your field. It's good to attend these just to network and get ideas, but you could also connect with someone in your industry who is more experienced and is willing to share some advice.
- Indirect Competitors can be a valuable source of knowledge. They won't feel threatened by your company, as you're not directly competing with them. They will still be familiar with your industry, and can give you advice

about targeting certain populations and what's going on in the market. Choose an established, noncompetitive company in your field that has had some success and reach out to their CEO.

- Volunteering at an organization related to your industry can help you to network with some key players. It could also bring you into contact with potential mentors, and show that you care enough to give back.[1]

Start by reaching out to successful leaders in your new industry. Ask the leader for 15 minutes over the phone and take the time to ask thoughtful questions and follow up with an authentic thank you note. People truly enjoy talking about themselves and what they do, so if you are respectful and appreciative you might be able to get a follow-up meeting and a mentor/mentee relationship can successfully begin. Just be sure not to inundate people with requests for time.

Before you talk to your mentor, you should have some questions ready to ask them. Some questions you can ask a mentor would include:

- What were some of the best things you did when you bought or started your business?
- What were some mistakes you made that you wish you had done differently?
- What were some of your strengths when you started out? What areas did you have to grow in?
- What are some important lessons you've learned over the years?
- How/When did you know that your business was in a good place and you were going to be successful?
- What are some resources I should use?
- How can I learn how to do   ?
- Do you have a method for managing a team? For planning?

As you develop a relationship with your mentor, you should share with them about your business: the challenges you are facing and the decisions you need to make. As your mentor learns more about you and your business, you can ask your mentor to be a sounding board for new ideas, and to help you see yourself more clearly as a leader.

Some questions you might want to ask your mentor about yourself as a leader once you've gotten to know each other include:

- What do you think are some of my strengths and weaknesses as a leader?
- What do you think I could do more of, or less of, to be successful?
- What impression have you gotten about my personality?
- How do you think I am coming across as a salesperson, leader, and boss?

You can also ask your mentor about specific situations that arise, where you're not sure what to do or you want to get a second opinion.[2]

Establish a Board

Before you panic about setting up a board, please realize that not everyone will need one. A board is not necessary, in fact they aren't necessary in many cases, but for other companies it can be incredibly beneficial. There is also a fine line between having a few mentors and developing a formal board. Most of the time, in the beginning, you can define that line on your own.

As you are working with your mentors and asking them questions about the business that you are running, you might find that it's easier to develop more parameters around a board. You might decide to have three members, or eight, or fifteen. You might give weekly, monthly, or quarterly reports.

You want a collection of people who will be a sounding board for you and will share their experiences and their contacts. You want a group that will help you find good people and help you find the right strategic direction for your business.[3]

You can find board members in much the same way that we have talked about finding mentors: through your existing contacts and LinkedIn. Search for people who could be a diverse sounding board to the business that you want to begin. You can create a job description and statement of qualifications for your board members so you are all on the same page for what to expect.[4] In the beginning you can ask for time with a small monetary contribution or gift, but as your company grows and moves along, you will most likely need to start some type of compensation, such as a small quarterly payment or rolled equity in the event that your business is sold.

If you are able to grow your business and if you do decide to accept any outside funding, you will most likely be required to have a board or to assign some of your seats to the organization responsible for the funding.

What Does the Board Do?

A board will help to make decisions for the company based on the interests of its shareholders. If you have investors at any point, you might want to offer them a position on the board. You will also want to have some internal managers from your corporation on the board, so that the board stays in touch with what is actually going on within the company.

Other types of decisions the board will have to make include:

- Hiring or firing executives
- Creating and amending dividend and options policies
- How much the executives are paid
- Setting corporate goals
- Providing support for the executives

- Overseeing the management of resources

The kinds of decisions a board can make, and how the board falls in the structure of an organization, are determined by its bylaws. Bylaws will also determine how many people are on the board, how often the board should meet, and how board members are elected or removed.[5]

Test Your Product or Service

Beyond getting mentors and potentially a board to give you feedback, a major aspect you need to do is test your product or service with your audience. A huge part of what you are going to do is to start making a name for yourself, and one of the best ways that you can do this is through testing your product/service onto the market for real feedback. Remember, good feedback is going to help your reputation. When someone uses a product or service that they love, they are going to tell others.

You should think about your audience, which we have devoted an entire chapter to later in the book. Who do you want to sell to? Who do you have experience selling to? And don't wrinkle your nose at the word "sell." Even though you are removed from your audience by a computer screen, you will become the lead salesperson for your company as its founder. Think about your audience. It is usually faster to sell to businesses because you can more easily and quickly reach them. But it is fun to have a consumer-focused concept that can be enjoyed by many. Spend time talking to your potential customers and understanding their pain.

Then, you need to get to the testing phase. If you have a product, it is crucial that you test it before you put it on the market. You'll save yourself a lot of time and money that you might have to spend down the road on recalling a product or issuing refunds.

When you do product testing, you are doing valuable

research. You need to gather insights about your consumers, such as the amount they might use your product, what their preferences about your product are, and any reactions they have to it, good or bad. The goal is to have people use your product and then collect their feedback through one of two methods: the In-Home Usage Test (IHUT) or the Central Location Test (CLT).

The In-Home Usage Test (IHUT)

The IHUT is useful for products that will be shipped to your customers' homes. You ship the product to a potential customer, and have them provide feedback.

Products that you may want to use this method for include anything that a consumer would need to use over a period of time to observe the results and give valuable feedback, such as hygiene products. This is most commonly used and, chances are, as a CEO this is the method you will use.

The Central Location Test (CLT)

The CLT is useful for products that you need to see in use to see how the consumer interacts with it. These are conducted in a controlled environment, such as a laboratory. Products that you may want to use this method with include ones that you want to test certain safety features on, or need to observe real-time footage of it being used by someone to know if it needs to be tweaked.

Goals of Product Testing

Before you begin product testing, make sure you set out clear goals and gather questions to ask your product testers that will help you achieve those goals.

One of the questions you are investigating in this stage is: does my product do what I claim it does? If not, how can it be improved to perform that function?

Or, you might want to think about whether your product is doing something other than its intended purpose, or could be applied in a different way. There are many examples of a product failing to be accepted for its intended purpose, and then being used for a different purpose instead. Bubble wrap, for example, was originally pitched as an idea for wallpaper. Viagra was first created as a blood pressure medication. Coca-Cola was invented as a way to help battle morphine addiction in the late 1800s, as morphine addiction had become a social issue due to its use as a painkiller.[6]

Consider All Feedback

You'll want to have consumers test out other aspects, once you have solidified the design of your product, such as the product packaging, the product appearance, and any initial impressions they get without using the product. This will help you to tweak how you are presenting your product.

Then, ask consumers to compare your product to other products and provide honest feedback. Would they purchase your product over the competitors'? Why or why not?[7]

Don't disregard feedback that isn't corroborated by others. Every piece of feedback is valuable, as it can give you an insight into your consumer's perspective.

Do Your Market Research

We spoke before about marketing research but want to address it again because it will help ensure that you are offering something that people will want or need. There are several ways that you can start doing primary market research, including reaching out to friends and family, doing online surveys, or working with social media.

One of the best ways to start market research is with your friends and family. Friends and family will usually offer you their time and opinion for free, as long as you don't inundate them with requests. You can ask a broad age range of friends and family to give opinions as they will help you decide on a demographic. You can ask them all sorts of questions, including their ideas for a price point, their need of the product, and where you should advertise. Friends and family are a great source because if they're excited about your product or service they will make sure their contacts are fired up for what you're putting out on the market.

Online surveys are a great way to gather primary market research. You can use a company like Survey Monkey, which offers analytics tools within their surveys to give you an insight into the reaction to your product or service. You can buy email lists to send the survey to or research online different people who might be able to give you good feedback. You need to get creative in offering an incentive for giving feedback as people who randomly receive a survey from you might be disinclined to give you any advice.

Social media is a great tool to gather a lot of information about the product or service that you want to launch. People are going to give fairly honest opinions through Facebook, Instagram, Twitter, TikTok and other platforms. If you want responses on social media you can advertise for people to respond, which will cost you money, or you can put it out there as a post or video. Just be sure to be genuine in what you put out there.

Testing a Product

Let's get into the specific detail of testing a product. While you can be almost positive about how popular your product is going to be, you still need to test it and then listen. Start by getting it into the hands of what you think is the target demographic. You would be surprised at how many people are willing to test a product for their review and their comments. But, how do you do this?

You might end up starting your business with a testing phase, where you could offer your product or services at a discounted rate in exchange for customer feedback. You want to find people who are unbiased and fit the profile of the type of customer you are trying to reach. You can find these customers at events where your product or service is relevant, through an online marketplace or service.

Additionally, you could offer a product or service at either a severely discounted rate or for free in exchange for some great customer reviews. This will set you up well when you are ready to launch because you can provide potential customers with the assurance that somebody had a good experience with your business.

Their feedback can help you figure out a couple things. First, you will know whether the group of people you are trying to target really want what you are offering. Second, you can gather feedback from them that will help you to improve your product. Third, you have made some connections. Those customers, if they showed interest, may be people you want to connect with in the future for feedback or help you to spread the word about your business.

After testing, you may feel like you're ready to launch, but you can't scale or provide the needed product or service to satisfy your future customers if you don't have the cash on the front end.

How can you get people to test your product? There are several ways you can do this. Here are a few ideas that you can use:

1. Put it on your website that you are looking for product testers. Have a simple form that they can fill out that includes their contact information, their age, and maybe even occupation if you are interested in a certain occupation for the target demographic.
2. Advertise on your social media channels that you are

looking for product testers. They get the product for free with the understanding that they provide honest reviews of the product that you can use for your own marketing.

3. If your product is going to target your local community, then walk around and approach strangers for testing this product.

Be sure that you have some method of collecting the comments and reviews that these people are giving you. A questionnaire with a comment section for their ultimate review is going to be a great start. Remember, if you receive some criticism, this is a part of the deal. Almost no one ever gets 100% satisfaction on their products. It could always be that the product tester really wasn't a fit to the target demographic, or you may have just been unlucky enough to get someone who always has something negative to say.

Testing Your Service

When you offer a service, it is a bit harder to test it on the market. However, you can still do your market research, which should give you an idea of who would be interested in the service that you are offering. One idea that you can try is to offer your services at a discounted rate to a group in order to get reviews. However, you have to decide if this is going to pay you in the long run. You don't want to give away the services for free ... you have put time and money into developing your business.

With a service, a big part of testing this is your market research and what you have found from those that you polled or interviewed. However, we do suggest that you get some reviewer feedback if at all possible when you do get people using your services. This can allow you to share your reviews with others, helping your credibility in what you offer.

Secondary Market Research

As you collect your primary market research you will turn to what is technically called secondary market research. In reality there won't be much of a line between these two methods, whereas secondary market research is looking at and analyzing the data that you received from all the above-mentioned methods. You will also sound more credible in an upcoming meeting when you use the term secondary market research. You might also be finishing up any research you did online or through phone calls on the industry. You will want to put together a competitive analysis, pricing analysis, and target audience, but don't get too caught up in these details as you mainly need to focus on starting.

Try not to skip the feedback stage, whether it be getting advice from mentors, board members, or potential customers. If you just ask a few people and roll with it, you will be getting started quicker but you might be missing out on opinions that could improve your business. Likewise, if you don't look into the competition, then you could be missing out on a different target demographic or higher price point that might mean all the difference in the world. Stay humble and listen as you gather this great feedback.

Chapter 5 Key Takeaways

After reading this chapter, what should you understand?

1. It is important to gain feedback through mentors, potentially a board of directors, and testing your product or service with your audience.
2. Mentors are critical for any CEO from home as they provide contacts and a fast track in your industry.
3. It is vital that you do your market research. How will you do this? Will you use online focus groups or ask individuals on your own?

4. Market research is key to how you will sell your product or service.

5. For product testing, discover ways to get people to interact, such as offering the product for free.

Endnotes

1   "10 Places to Find Mentors and Advisors for Entrepreneurs." Accessed September 5, 2020. https://www.entrepreneur.com/article/271908

2   Jo Miller. "40 Questions To Ask A Mentor." Accessed September 5, 2020. https://www.forbes.com/sites/jomiller/2018/03/25/40-questions-to-ask-a-mentor/#2f3f3cb8261b

3   Anna Meyer. "How COVID-19 Will Shape Holiday Retail Shopping in 2020." Accessed October 7, 2020. https://www.inc.com/anna-meyer/holiday-retail-shopping-trends-2020.html

4   Terry Masters. "How to Put Together a Board of Directors." Accessed October 7, 2020. https://smallbusiness.chron.com/put-together-board-directors-41962.html

5   James Chen. "Board of Directors (B of D)." Accessed September 5, 2020.

6   Will Heilpern. "11 famous products that were originally intended for a completely different purpose." https://www.businessinsider.com/successful-products-that-were-originally-intended-for-a-completely-different-purpose-2016-3#coca-cola-started-out-as-a-cure-for-morphine-addiction-1

7   Çağlar Bozkurt. "Product Testing Research: A Step by Step Guide." Accessed September 5, 2020. https://www.twentify.com/blog/product-testing-research-a-step-by-step-guide

Chapter 6

Find Good People

Finding talented and motivated people to come along with you as a CEO from home is unbelievably important. No matter which CEO type you are and what business you are operating, the entity you're running is only as strong, efficient, and successful as the people who help do its work and keep customers and other team members inspired. Your people are the most important part of what you do.

Making the wrong hire in the early stages of a business can cost you time, money, and emotional strain. A study conducted by CB Insights showed that making bad hires early on was the third reason given by startups for why they didn't succeed.[1] Even if your company is off to a good start, you want to be careful that you don't make the wrong choice of whom you hire.

Making the right choice in hiring can give your company the momentum it needs and its enviable edge. Most importantly, it can help you sleep better at night. You want the people on your team to bring positive energy, excitement for growth, and a healthy work environment that others will be excited to join. Don't be afraid to eliminate someone who is working against your vision of the organization. You can coach someone out of your organization by giving adequate warnings through regular feedback and having conversations that help to move them to their next opportunity.

Before we get into all the technical points and ideas about finding talent, we should talk about the most important tools for recruiting people, including your ingenuity, persuasion, and hustle. You can spend all the time in the world putting together the perfect job description but nothing will replace the heart and soul that you feel for what you have created. Make sure this comes through loud and clear with whomever you recruit to work with you. Be authentic in your discussions about your vision and what you want to create and likeminded people will be drawn to you.

Try to start with sweat equity in the hiring process before spending money with recruiters or recruitment websites. Remember the feedback sources we talked about in the last chapter? Use your mentors, board members, and those you asked for opinions to put you in touch with others who might want to help. Put out feelers on social media and LinkedIn. Whenever you are on the phone or talking with someone in person, ask them for someone they could refer you to. Challenge yourself to hustle and find creative ways to get the best people. For instance, in the beginning at Salesboxer we needed to hire writers so we went to university newspapers online, looked for bylines, and emailed those students to ask if they were interested in an internship. In another instance at Salesboxer, we worked with a university program that offered their students' time and skills for free to develop video content.

As an entrepreneur forging ahead you might want to consider doing a job for some period of time before you hire someone else to do it. Doing the job first has several benefits. First, you have better knowledge of what the job requires and the right person to fill it. Second, you can better judge if the person is efficient in their work. Finally, it saves money in the short term. We are big fans of delegating, and it's critical to growing your endeavor, so you want to find the right balance between your time and developing mastery for the job in order to hire the best person.

Assess Your Needs: What Kind of Talent Do You Need?

Depending on what type of business you are running from home, you will have different talent needs. If you are investing in property, you might not need to make direct hires but will need to find the best contractors and property managers you can find. If you are launching a product, you will need a manufacturing team. If you are working as a gig owner CEO or absentee owner CEO, you will want to find the best in your specialty who are potentially working as independent consultants. Regardless of what CEO type you are, you will most likely need a web developer or graphic design person to put together the visual representation for your company. We will focus a lot in this chapter on the active owner CEO, because your hiring needs, at least in the beginning, will be the greatest. However, all businesses, business types, and CEO types can benefit from the ideas set forth in this chapter.

There are several different options you should consider before you begin planning to recruit talent. You will want to ask yourself:

Do I need long-term or short-term, gig-based talent?

Is it better for me to hire an employee or an independent contractor? This will depend on whether you have ongoing projects you'll need a point person for, or whether you don't know what you'll need. Consider the benefits and risks: freelance, gig-based talent can get pulled to other companies and projects, and they may not be as invested in your company as a more permanent hire. On the other hand, you can pay them for a project or two and then move on if you don't have continuing needs in that area. If your company needs someone who will understand your vision inside and out and be fully invested, then you'll want to consider making a more long-term hire.

Do I need someone local or can I use a remote worker?

Do you need someone you can meet in-person at a local coffee shop or at your home, or are you fine with remote communication and collaboration? A remote hire is a great option for startups, as it expands your pool of candidates and means you can find someone who lives in an area of the country where the cost of living is lower and could, therefore, accept lower pay. Hiring someone who you are geographically close to can help deepen the bond and culture of what you are trying to create.

Do I want to hire people one at a time or would it benefit me to work with a recruiter or staffing group?

A recruiter or staffing group tends to be more expensive to work with, but they'll get the job done more quickly and professionally. It's less expensive to hire individuals, however, and that allows you to handpick the type of talent for your company.

What are the costs of making this hire?

You'll need to consider the cost of any websites, resources, and personnel expended to recruit great talent. You'll have to factor in the salary and benefits you'll offer, any extra tax fees, and the cost of training.[2]

What are the financial benefits this hire would bring me?

How would hiring someone increase your sales, allow you to expand, or take tasks off the plate of a higher-paid or overtaxed employee?

Human Resources Is Critical to Your Business

In the beginning of your business you will hire people to fill roles that you simply cannot do on your own. You might be contracting with other firms, hiring independent contractors, or bringing on full-time, part-time or intern-level labor. You will need to put together best practices to follow for the human resources element of your business.

You might be lucky enough to find yourself with your own

in-house human resources partner, but in almost every case, you will be wearing that important hat from day one. Simply put, various local, regional and national governments have rules for employers to follow and it becomes very costly for you not to follow them. For example, you can use independent consultant help, and we recommend it, but in the US you need to make sure that you are paying someone's employer identification number (EIN) at tax time and not their individual social security number to be compliant and not risk an audit. You also need to ensure that the independent consultant works with others to be considered a true consultant.

Human resources is useful to you in many aspects of hiring employees and managing their work in your organization. You will want to be sure your offer letters, employee handbook, payroll, benefits, insurance and more aspects of human resources are all working to your favor. You can do this internally if you have the knowledge. You can hire a human resources outsourcing group to guide you. HR outsourcing is broken down into ASOs, administrative services organizations, and PEOs, professional employer organizations. They do some of the same things, but a PEO is your employer of record. An ASO will in many cases do more for you and if you use an ASO your business will be able to develop a health insurance history over time and will have more flexibility, which is something that a PEO can't offer. You will make the best decision for your company.

Look Online for Talent

In the age of working remotely, talent has never been easier to find online. Once you start looking for ways to connect with the talented individuals you want to recruit, however, the plethora of options can become overwhelming.

Here are some places you might want to start. Many of these are freelance job sites, job boards, and ways to connect with companies.

Toptal
- Prescreened, top technical talent
- Free matching with candidates by a live recruiter
- More expensive hourly rate

Penji
- Unlimited graphic design service
- Monthly cost ($369/month)

Onlinejob.ph
- Great virtual assistants
- Wide range of skills
- Low-cost

99 Designs
- Make a design contest with graphic designers competing to win your project
- Clear and organized process for job posting

GitHub
- Online gathering place for tech talent
- Network online to find good tech talent

Fiverr
- Hire freelancers for $5 gigs such as finding keywords
- Variety of projects and freelancers[8]

Upwork
- Variety of skills
- Agencies and freelancers
- Easy to track job progress
- Financial protection for clients and freelancer
- Can pay by the hour or a flat fee by the project

LinkedIn

- Free to set up a company page
- Link employees with company page to expand your network
- Target talent with job postings
- LinkedIn Recruiter, Recruiter Lite and LinkedIn Profinder help connect you with talent[9]

AngelList

- Social recruiting tool through networking
- Make a company page
- Post jobs for free on job boards
- Used to hire for tech and remote positions for startups[10]

FlexJobs.com

- Unlimited job posting and resume searches
- Geo-targeting
- Applicant Tracking System (ATS)
- Upgrade options such as virtual job fairs, webinars, and targeted e-blasts

Craigslist

- Free or $7–75 to post jobs, depending on the area
- Paid posting account provides management tools, online payments, and more[11]

Scripted

- Hire vetted writers for content, copywriting, SEO, social media, and more
- Read samples to help you choose a freelancer
- Plans start at $149/month[12]

Indeed, Glassdoor, Monster and CareerBuilder

- Keep tabs on open, paused, and closed jobs and those

who've applied to them
- Keep track of how many people have applied
- Preview overview of applicants

WPHired.com and Jobs.WordPress.net
- Job boards to reach WordPress talent
- Find WordPress developers for plugins, content, photoshopped files and more
- Free to post jobs

Contently
- Global freelance content network
- Over 140,000 writers, editors, filmmakers, designers, etc.
- Top talent from popular publications
- Talent matching algorithm

In addition to these platforms, you can tap into various networks that you may already have or are easy to access.

Tell Your Friends

You are not coming to the journey of being a CEO from home in a bubble. You can draw from years of being around people plus your professional experiences and schooling. For example, in your friends' groups on Facebook, your professional groups on LinkedIn or other social media, or through organizations you are a part of, you can spread the word about the type of talent you want to attract. The old methods of networking, by telling friends and family, can be just as helpful as those online, especially if you're looking for local talent. You should spread the word through your online friends as well. Social media can help get people's attention.

In the past 20 years, there has been an increase in specialty groups online. One example are mom groups. These moms might want the flexibility to work from home, yet have education, talent, and experience that would make them valuable assets. This makes it the perfect talent network to tap into, through CircleofMoms.com, CafeMom.com, Mothers & More, and Mocha Moms, Inc.

You can also connect with talented moms who are looking for remote work through The Mom Project (https://themomproject.com), which connects educated, talented, experienced women with top-level employers who advocate for a good work/life balance. Similarly, HireMyMom.com connects small businesses with North American competent professionals who are mothers.

Use Learning Platforms

Online learning platforms can be a good source of talent. The savvy worker will be continually training themselves to be better at what they do. They will frequent information-rich websites such as Medium, to gain ideas and share some of their own. If you join and start reading articles from people who are writing the kind of content you need for your business, you can easily connect with them and offer them a gig or a job.

Connect with Training and Educational Programs

You can connect with internship programs, apprenticeship programs, and vocational high schools in your area, as high schoolers and college students can be great people to hire. Even though they might not have years of experience, they have a greater sense of how to connect with younger people and are usually very open to learning new skills. Plus their excitement and idealism can be an untapped treasure for your vision.

You can build relationships with schools that have such programs available to students. By the time these students have become skilled and graduate, you'll get first dibs if you already have this ongoing relationship with the school.

Additionally, you will want to plug into job fairs, which

are offered online and in person. Some of the online job fairs include GarysGuide and Uncubed Daily.[14]

Consider being a mentor for a university, too. For example, if you connect with the professor of web design at your local community college, something your at-home business specializes in, students who graduate from that program will already know about your business and the professor can recommend you to other students. Additionally, you can partner with the university through the career service platform, Handshake, to recruit fresh talent from universities that specialize in training students in your area of business.

Use Social Media

Don't simply tell people on social media that you're hiring. Start showing off you, your team, how much fun you're having, and why your brand and vision are the best. Show off the talent of your employees and give them shout-outs. When people see positive, fun, inspiring posts, they'll be more inclined to not only follow your business but want to work there. You'll attract talented individuals who want to work for your company and who are intrinsically motivated to get the job done.

Invest in Each Employee

With each person who starts to work with you, take the time to really get to know them, work with them, and make them feel part of the team. When your employees genuinely like working for you, they'll let others know, without you needing to prompt them. When others see their social media posts about how they love their job or hear about it over coffee, they'll want to be in on the fun.[15]

When others hear of a need to fill a position, it's not as compelling as hearing about the passion and vision behind an organization. Spread the word about why your business matters through guest blogging on other people's sites and blogs. Speak at a conference. Offer video tutorials related to your product or service. Build the excitement about your business and the right people will begin to find you.

Sarah Hum from the small product feedback business, Canny, shared in a blog post on their website that they never set out to attract new employees through their blog and Instagram, but that's exactly what ended up happening. People saw the good time their team was having in the lively photos on Instagram, which showcased the personalities of the teammates.

On her blog and Instagram feed, Hum showed simple, organic content commenting on Canny's journey as a startup. The type of people they would want to hire were attracted to their content and sent in applications. They have made several successful hires this way.[16]

Always Be Hiring

Remember to always be hiring, whether at a coffee shop, remote or in-person conference, and on social media. You never know when you will need someone, and quick. If you continually have your feelers out there, you will have plenty of talented candidates on hand when a critical need arises.

If someone great applies for a job, but you end up going with someone else, you can keep their information on file and connect with them on occasion. Then, when you need to make another hire, you won't have to repeat the entire recruiting process.

Make a Recruiting Plan

You will always want to be deliberate about making the right hires. This can be a plan on an Excel sheet or something you've put together in an email. It doesn't matter how informal or formal the plan is, just be thoughtful about when and if you need people.

Go ahead and make profiles of the skills, character, and personality the people should possess to be successful in working alongside you.[3] Next, you'll need to find the talent to fit these profiles, based on what you can reasonably offer them. The types of skills you are looking for and what you are able to pay will help you determine where to search. Before you begin searching, you should have an interview process in mind so that you have the next steps in place once you find talented people you might want to hire. The interview process you come up with should include a clear discussion of the job description, expectations, and benefits, so there is less confusion when they start working.[4]

For example, let's say you are starting a floral delivery service from home. You have gotten some great vendors on board, drawn up a business plan, secured funding, and are ready to start the hiring process.

You know you'll want to hire people who, like you, are passionate about delivering flowers on time to customers who want to honor special people in their lives. You look over your business plan and discover you'll need to hire some savvy tech support for the website, a content writer for the blog, and a social media manager.

You're not sure how long you will need the tech support, so you decide to hire a freelancer. You know you'll want ongoing content for your blog and social media, so you combine the two, deciding to look for someone who can do both kinds of content.

Before you can make an accurate job description, visualize who you will need with you. You can brainstorm some candidate personas, detailing the skills, experience, personality, location, and availability of your ideal candidate. Then, you can even write out an employee value proposition, which spells out what this type of candidate will bring to your company as well as what your company has to offer that type of candidate. The value proposition will go a long way in helping define your brand and the overall culture of your company. Remember, even though you are working from home, you want to have a culture and idea that people can relate to when they work with you. The last thing you'll need to do to prepare for interviewing candidates is to create detailed job descriptions based on your employee value proposition and vision statement.

Once you've outlined and started advertising a position, you will start to receive and assess resumes. Do they have spelling and grammatical errors? What kinds of companies has the candidate worked for? Do they have work experience that directly relates to what you are looking for? Here are some ideas in evaluating the resumes:[5]

- Look for job stability in their history, with bonus points for an internal promotion
- Look for a record of achievement, and make sure it is legitimate
- Look for cultural fit with what you are putting together
- Make sure their work experience either directly or indirectly relates to what you do

In your interview, you will need to dig a little deeper and ask open-ended, probing questions about them, such as "Tell me about your experience working for your previous company?" or "What made you leave your job at this place?" If you are new to interviewing, you might find yourself surprisingly as nervous as the candidate. That's normal. Just jump right in and get to work getting to know the person. Experienced interviewers are looking for what they aren't answering, the questions they aren't asking, and their subtle tone of voice and responses. Here are some ideas for questions you can ask:[6]

- What three words would you use to describe your ideal job?
- Can you name a skill that you would use to do this job

well?
- What professional achievement are you most proud of?
- What type of boss is your favorite?
- Can you describe your own working style?

And also, a couple of questions to hire for a remote worker:[7]

- Do you have a hard time setting you own schedule and staying disciplined?
- Are you self-motivated, and can you give me an example?

Some other important points to consider as you go through the interview process:

- Is this person responsive and responsible? If you are hiring remotely, the person must be highly responsive. This will also communicate a sense of responsibility. Everyone is busy, but chances are, if they respond to your messages within 24 hours or less, they are responsible as well.
- Does this person seem interested in and motivated about your business? Look at what the person said about their interest in your *business*, not just the job, in their application. You can't afford to hire someone who isn't motivated by what you are trying to do.
- Does this person's personality fit the business culture and brand I am building?[17] If your business is light-hearted and fun, you'll want to hire people who embody that. On the other hand, if your business is all about being tech nerds (think Geeksquad), you'll want to hire people who can embody and sell that brand based on their personality.
- Is this person dynamic and teachable? You need people who are able to switch gears and work on different kinds of projects or aspects of a project. You can't hire a bunch of genius specialists right away. You need people who are

willing to learn how to do things as they go, as you can't always predict what your startup will require in its early stages.

- Is this person a go-getter? You need people who are confident and willing to take initiative as your company gets off the ground. You have your fingers in many different pies at the moment and you can't take your foot off the gas to babysit your new employee. You need people who will take what instruction you're able to give them and run with it, creating and doing things to make your business succeed.

- Does this person have previous experience working for a startup or small business? People who understand the startup game will be more reasonable in their expectations about what your company can offer them. They'll understand that their role will include wearing many hats and will possibly morph over time. Additionally, all businesses start small, so someone with experience working for a smaller business could be a good candidate as well.

- How much experience does this person bring? A couple of years of experience may be all you need, and all you want, to hire your candidate. If they are very experienced, they may ask for more compensation and benefits than you can give them.

Apogee CEO Andre Zafrani says that he looks for disciplined, self-motivated and hard-working people when he hires people to work remotely.

Finally, and we know this from experience, check at least two references. The references seem like overkill but they are so necessary. If a candidate refuses to give you references, this is a bad sign. If a reference gives you a curt, lukewarm answer, this is also a bad sign. You can be brief with a reference check but ask questions like "Would you hire this person again?" or

"What did this person bring to the table?" You will be very happy to have checked references because they oftentimes come true, both good and bad.

How to Convince Talent to Work with You

When you've identified the candidates you are going to move forward with and start the interview process, you may find that you need to incentivize the best talent to convince them to work for you. After all, they're taking a risk. How can they be sure that your small business is going to make it? Why should they work for your growing company instead of a larger, more established one?

You need to figure out what your company can offer them that is comparable, or even better, than a well-established brand. You may not be able to compete with the pay and benefits, but there are plenty of other incentives you can offer your dream employees.

Be Creative in How You Pay

Be sure to emphasize what is unique about your company.[18] If the talent you are looking to recruit turns out to be someone looking to build their resume and skills in their field (and it should!), then you will want to sell them on the idea that this job will offer them unique challenges and skill acquisition they won't find other places. For a young, entrepreneurial candidate, this could be the selling point that gets them in the door.

You can offer stock options, or equity in the business, to offset lower pay, but try to stay away from this option, as you want to save the equity for when you might need it most. Up front this may not seem like the most tempting option, but if someone is genuinely interested in working for your company, they'll see the future value of what you're offering and appreciate the effort in compensating them well.

As previously discussed, people are drawn to a positive

work environment where others have had a good experience. If you can get your happy employees to share testimonials on Indeed and other job boards, people will be more willing to take a little bit of a pay cut to work in an environment they think they'll enjoy.

You can offer authority in their area, so they are able to discover and promote their own expertise. They say flattery will get you everything, and in this case it can go a long way towards getting you a talented employee. If you show that you value their skills and experience in a field by telling them they'll have the freedom to do the job the way they want to, or that they will be the resident expert in their area (this can be conveyed in a job title such as "WordPress Expert"), they will be more inclined to take the position. Talented people like to be respected for their skill and to have the ability to use it authoritatively.

Offer Flexible Hours and Remote Work
The benefit of working from home is that you can offer flexible hours and a remote work option, which can outweigh lower pay. Remind your candidates of the benefits, including that this eliminates commute time and allows them to maintain a healthy work/life balance.

In Rare Cases, Give Them a Small Share in Your Company
As a small business, you have the option to offer candidates or employees a small share to help the business succeed. We recommend to keep this in your proverbial back pocket for as long as necessary and don't use it if you don't have to. However, equity in your business does ensure that your people will be personally invested in it.

Make Them Feel at Home
Whether you end up hiring someone or not, you want to make

sure the people working with you have the best experience possible. Making someone feel like their time and talent are respected will make them more inclined to listen to your offer. Remember, the interview process goes both ways, and candidates who feel uncomfortable in the hiring process may decide it's not worth working for a company that doesn't communicate clearly, efficiently, and warmly.

Develop a Framework

It is crucial to develop a framework for any business, most of all one where you are all working from home. Employees can develop deep-rooted anxiety of the unknown with their jobs if they don't have clearly defined goals that are reinforced often. The framework and goals will also give you opportunities for important reflection of the business and an ability to celebrate accomplishments.

Start your framework with an employee handbook that outlines all of the policies, benefits, and guidelines for your employees. You can look up examples online or get help from an HR outsourcing company. Be sure to include a mission, vision, company story, and statement of values. You as the CEO can't be a part of every conversation and meeting, so put these together so everyone will know where the company stands. You will want to refer back to the mission, vision, story and values often, so they become a living, breathing set of principles for everyone as they act on behalf of your company and your culture.

A framework for your people includes a solid onboarding process and training. Put together a robust offer letter that welcomes your new employee and outlines what you want people to know about your company. Make sure the offer letter includes statements about entering employment at will and gives you the ability as the manager to terminate employment. Flex HR provides example language, after your welcome and outline of any compensation, for your offer letter:

> Your employment with our company is voluntarily entered into and you are free to resign at any time for any reason. Similarly, the company has the right to terminate the employment relationship at any time for any reason. While we hope that our relationship will be mutually beneficial, the company can give no guarantee or contract, either express or implied, of continued employment.

Be sure to set up a training program that can be adapted for employees as the company grows. We recommend including things that new employees can read and items they can accomplish. In order to make it easier for hiring, give the new employee a set of tangible outcomes for each week, so it doesn't overly burden you or the hiring manager. You can get so many good ideas for people when they are new, optimistic, and see a future in your business. Capitalize on these ideas and make sure either a manager or you are around these new employees a lot in the beginning.

Your framework should include a set of meetings. We recommend a daily huddle call for 20 minutes each morning. It's a great way for your management team to connect and talk about the day ahead. You can also think about one-on-one meetings each week, a weekly strategic management team meeting, and yearly performance reviews. The meetings help alleviate anxiety for employees (and you) from the unknown and they also help establish and re-establish the culture that is critical for your business to succeed.

Finally, you will want your framework to include a process for termination. It is inevitable that certain employees will need to be terminated or they will voluntarily make the decision to move to another organization. Don't be afraid of these changes and instead embrace them. You can even create an alumni network for your organization to ease the departure of employees and ensure that no bridges are burned. In the case of a resignation, you will want to make sure you do an exit interview with the employee. In case of a termination, Brad Morehead, CEO of Assembly Healthcare, recommends documented warnings against performance and then in the case of letting them go, using the term, "This is your last day with the company," and outlining options for them, which ideally removes some of the hurt feelings. When someone resigns or is terminated, you should get ahead of the departure with your organization by announcing it yourself to the staff and controlling the narrative with a positive spin.

Make a Great Culture

If you are going to the trouble of hiring employees to carry out your vision, you want to be sure that they stay. The best way to ensure employee retention, and also to create passion about what you're doing with customers and employees alike, is to make a great culture within your company. There are exhaustive articles, books and research about great company cultures. You will need to get more creative when building a culture around a remote workforce, but it is entirely possible.

Robert Glazer, who is the founder and CEO of Acceleration Partners, a global partner marketing agency, provides a lot of tips for remote culture in his company of 177 employees. He says it's important to create a few times each year that everyone can get together in person, perhaps through an annual meeting and a few other in-person events.

Glazer also talks about leadership transparency as it relates to company culture. You can create very clear goals for each employee and track them together, so they get consistent feedback. You can also host virtual company town hall meetings where leadership will provide financial updates and strategic goals plus answer questions from all employees.[19] Plus, you can use Zoom, Microsoft Teams, or other technology tools to get everyone together virtually for fun, like playing trivia or games. Get creative and be authentic to your brand and your company.

Your people are your biggest asset as an entrepreneur and CEO from home. Be strategic from the beginning about all the people you choose to involve on your journey, as they will be the keys to your organization's success or failure. Educate yourself and hire experts to help you with human resources, as it is a critical component of the people part of your business. And be mindful to hire the right people, but only when you absolutely need the resources. Go it alone until you need to delegate and use the resources in this chapter to help you find and manage the right people.

Chapter 6 Key Takeaways

After reading this chapter, what should you understand?

1. Be mindful of the complexity and necessity of a good human resources strategy for your business and don't be afraid to outsource this to experts.
2. Use ingenuity, persuasion and hustle to find the right people.
3. Don't pay money for employees and people until you absolutely have to.
4. Do a job first before you hire someone to do it.
5. Choose the website or recruiting method that best fits the skills you need and the time, energy, and resources you have.
6. Develop your own interview and assessment process to make sure a candidate is the right fit.
7. Create a handbook and framework for your employees to continue to establish your company culture.

Endnotes

1   Anja Zojceska. "How to Successfully Hire for a Startup." Accessed April 21, 2020. https://www.talentlyft.com/en/blog/article/237/guide-how-to-successfully-hire-for-a-startup

2   "6 Great Recruitment Strategies For Startups." Accessed April 27, 2020. https://www.firstbird.com/en/magazine/6-great-recruitment-strategies-for-startups/

3   Michael Thompson. "5 Pro Startup Recruiting Tips to Attract Talent." Accessed April 21, 2020. https://about.crunchbase.com/blog/startup-recruiting-tips/

4   Bailey Reiners. "Maximize Your Startup Recruitment Efforts with These Seven Essential Tactics." Accessed April 27, 2020. https://builtin.com/recruiting/startup-recruitment

5   https://www.inc.com/david-finkel/6-keys-to-look-for-when-evaluating-the-resume-of-a-job-applicant.html

6   Kat Boogaard. "10 Best Questions to Ask an Interviewee." Accessed October 7, 2020. https://www.themuse.com/advice/top-10-questions-to-ask-an-interviewee

7   Robert Glazer. "I'm the CEO of a company with 177 employees that's been entirely remote for 13 years. Here are ways we built a thriving remote work culture." Accessed October 7, 2020. https://www.businessinsider.com/ceo-of-remote-company-5-ways-to-built-thriving-culture-2020-3#prioritize-professional-development-5

8   "7 Best Freelance Websites to Find Talent in 2020." Accessed April 21, 2020. https://ddiy.co/freelance-websites/

9   Gregory Lewis. "How Small Businesses Can Use LinkedIn to Recruit." Accessed April 23, 2020. https://business.linkedin.com/talent-solutions/blog/small-business/2017/how-small-businesse-can-use-linkedin-to-recruit

10   "AngelList Recruiting: How to Recruit Talent Free on AngelList." Accessed April 23, 2020. https://www.betterteam.com/angellist-recruiting

11 Taylor Cotter. "How to post jobs on Craigslist: A step-by-step guide for employers." Accessed April 23, 2020. https://resources.workable.com/tutorial/how-to-post-jobs-on-craigslist

12 "Grow Your Business." Accessed April 23, 2020. https://www.scripted.com/pricing-membership

13 "Using the Indeed Employer Dashboard to Manage Recruitment." Accessed April 23, 2020. https://www.indeed.com/hire/resources/howtohub/using-the-indeed-employer-dashboard-to-manage-recruitment

14 Ilya Pozin. "4 Places Startups Can Find the Talent They Need." Accessed April 21, 2020. https://www.inc.com/ilya-pozin/4-places-startups-can-find-talent-they-need.html

15 Bernhard Schroeder. "Nine Insights on How To Recruit And Keep The Right People For Your Company Or Startup." Accessed April 21, 2020. https://www.forbes.com/sites/bernhardschroeder/2019/12/13/nine-insights-on-how-to-recruit-and-keep-the-right-people-for-your-company-or-startup/#604981b02294

16 From: Sarah Hum. "How we've managed to attract top talent to our early-stage startup." Accessed April 21, 2020. https://canny.io/blog/startup-attract-top-talent/

17 Anja Zojceska. "How to Successfully Hire for a Startup." Accessed April 21, 2020. https://www.talentlyft.com/en/blog/article/237/guide-how-to-successfully-hire-for-a-startup

18 Craig Bloem. "How to Recruit Top Talent When No One's Heard of Your Startup." Accessed April 21, 2020. https://www.inc.com/craig-bloem/how-to-recruit-top-talent-when-no-ones-heard-of-your-startup.html

19 Robert Glazer. "I'm the CEO of a company with 177 employees that's been entirely remote for 13 years. Here are ways we built a thriving remote work culture." Accessed October 7, 2020. https://www.businessinsider.com/ceo-of-

remote-company-5-ways-to-built-thriving-culture-2020-3#prioritize-professional-development-5

Chapter 7

Market Your Business

Marketing your business encompasses all the ideas, culture, and energy about you and your company and displaying them together in the best light for your potential customers. This can be expressed in the words and images you use to depict your business, from your logo, to your name, to your website address, among a myriad of other things. You might be starting a business for college apartment rentals. You might be launching a flower delivery business. You might be running a medical billing company that you have taken from a traditional office to fully virtual. Regardless of what business you are starting or currently running, you will need a good marketing strategy.

The marketing exercise starts like this: What is your business going to be called? How are you going to brand yourself? What will be the company's website? Think which company names you immediately gravitate toward and think about those that are clumsy or awkward. You might find yourself on GoDaddy for hours trying to find the right name that is actually available. We would like to offer a shortcut piece of advice: don't get too wrapped up in the time and money of marketing your business. While branding is important, continuing to execute each day on your idea is more essential.

Think first about your customers before getting too caught up in the details of marketing. Once you attract your first customers it is crucial that they are delighted enough to tell more potential customers, and get the ball rolling for you. One of the best ways to build your reputation is through satisfying those first few customers and continuing to build upon this success.

A big part of marketing is getting a name for your company that is going to showcase who you are and what you bring to the market. It will differ for a variety of reasons, but chief among them is if you market your business to consumers or businesses. Along with getting the actual name and logo for your company, you also have to look at the branding of your company. How are you going to get your name out to the market? How are you going to build a reputation for your company? While you must continue to execute each day, marketing will be important for attracting more clients over time and truly turning your operation into a successful business.

Your Audience

Before we start with anything, let's take a moment and consider your audience. The first exercise is to divide audiences into two categories: consumers or decision-makers in a business. This is commonly referred to as B2C (business to customers) or B2B (business to business). Is yours B2B or B2C? You will generally need to spend a bit more time, money, and consideration on marketing if it's a B2C company. A B2B audience is usually more targeted.

Next, can you describe your ideal customer? Start with age, gender, geography, income level, and interests. Who has access to large numbers of your ideal customer? Perhaps Facebook does, if you're targeting women who are 30–64 years old. Maybe it's LinkedIn or the executive directors of chambers of commerce, if you're targeting the owners of businesses. Maybe your customers are on TikTok or Reels, if you're trying to find a younger audience. Keep this audience in mind as you develop the marketing elements for your business.

Picking Your Name

As we previously mentioned, it can be tempting to spend days, weeks, and even months trying to think of the perfect name for your business. For some people, they get the name immediately. Other times, it is not quite so easy. The worse thing that you can do is to spend so much time on the name that you let the idea of your business float from one month or year to the next. Consider this, did you know that Groupon was originally called ThePoint? OpenTable was originally called Easy Eats. These examples show that the name can change if something comes up. So, don't stress over the name so much that you start letting other issues slip through the cracks.

Since you are picking a name, remember that your website should be one that has the name in it. It's also helpful for a sparkling new business in the large world of the Internet to have words that indicate what it does in the title, website address, or subheadings. Be mindful of the words you use because it will lend you more credibility and make it easier for people to find you and your website.

Knowing what your business is going to offer will help you choose the right name. It's also why this chapter falls toward the middle of the book, after you have identified a lot of pieces of your business. For example, a company that is working with estate sales will want to have their location and the phrase "estate sales" included in their name to make them easier to find. Likewise, a company that is offering hair care products may want to include a keyword like "healthy hair" in their title, depending upon what type of products they are offering.

The keyword tool that Google provides can be a great free tool to look at what people are searching when they are looking for a company that may offer your future services. Google can be a great starting point with figuring out what your company name should be, or narrowing down your options. The keyword tool will aid in good SEO practices for your business, which is one element that will help you be found online.

We have some pointers for what the name should be:

- Make it easy to spell and pronounce
- Make it meaningful to you

- Make sure it is available within the state where you are registering your business entity
- It's nice if the name somehow tells a story about what you do
- Ensure there is some form of website address available to include your name

How do you think of a name? We have some thoughts:[1]

- Ask your friends and family members
- Do a stream of consciousness exercise where you spend 20 minutes writing down words that come to your mind when describing your business
- Look up synonyms of words that describe your business
- Think of words that have been meaningful in the past to you that may come from literature, movies, or the arts
- Think of a street, last name, or family symbol that is meaningful
- Use a play on words to convey what you do
- Use resources available for generating a name like Shopify Business Name Generator, NameMesh.com, or Naminum. com
- You could use a non-English word, but please be careful as you don't want to unknowingly use cultural appropriation
- If you have acquired a business, consider keeping its name

Getting the Logo

Once you have your company name, the next step is your logo. Honestly, while the name is sometimes a difficult exercise, getting the logo is usually more fun. The logo is a visual representation of your entire concept taken from a bird's-eye view. As you decide on a logo, it can help you think through the essential elements of what your business is about. A logo lends you a lot of credibility. Just by sending an email with your logo at the bottom, sending a PDF with your logo, or creating a simple website with a professional logo in the corner, you are signaling to others that you are serious about what you are doing.

A good place to start for creating a logo is Crowdspring, which crowd-sources graphic designers who will submit their ideas. You can usually get a logo done for around $400 and within seven days.

However, for those who have a little creativity and are interested in trying to save as much money as they can, they can use Canva or another graphic design platform to help them create a logo completely on their own. A few tips include:

- Certain colors look better when combined. Do you recall what your art teacher taught you as a child? There are complementary colors that work better together.
- There is a science behind colors. For example, red is considered sexy and invigorating, blue is considered professional, orange is considered energetic, and brown is considered to be steady. What is your color choice saying about your business?
- Be unique in what you design. You do not want this logo to be similar to something else in your industry or in general. Not only is this not helping you to stand out in the crowd, but you could have legal issues if you were to duplicate a popular logo.
- Get feedback. Mock up a few designs to show around and let them decide which ones look the best and what you should decide on.
- Make a logo that is easy to draw on a sheet of paper. Make sure your logo is simple enough that a child could draw it on a sheet of paper.

And remember, your logo may not be the next Apple or Nike. It took years and a lot of marketing for these businesses to have a logo that was recognized on sight. Your goal is to have a logo that can be associated with your brand and make it look professional and recognizable.

Make No Small Plans

Daniel Burnham was talking about Chicago when he said those four words, but making no small plans can certainly be applied to your new company's marketing. Your marketing plan can be as simple as an email sent to yourself or notes in your phone, or you could take the time to put it in a PowerPoint presentation (which we would not advise). Don't get bogged down in details, whatever you do, but make sure you have ideas for what to do and how to tell your company's story.

You can start with the acronym SMART that helps you give a framework to your marketing goals. You want your goals to be:

- Specific
- Measurable
- Achievable
- Realistic
- Time-bound

Create a detailed overview of your marketing strategies with corresponding tactics of how you will execute them. Let's say you want to grow your customer base by 30 percent throughout the first quarter of the fiscal year. You might identify one of your tactics as creating a targeted email list of your prospects, and market to them with a weekly newsletter. Perhaps you also identify Google AdWords and social media as a three-pronged effort to attract customers and grow sales. The Google keyword tool we talked about before or trending topics on Instagram and Twitter can show you ways to capture customer demand for your business.

Be sure to have some ideas around the investment you need to successfully get the word out about your new business. Look for any inexpensive alternatives and ways that you can use your own creativity and hustle as a replacement for dollars. What type of money and time will be required for the goals and tactics you identified? Your marketing activities will most likely start with paid lead sources, public relations, social media, email marketing, and guerrilla marketing tactics, so we will start here with tactics and details.

Paid Lead Sources

Regardless of what business you are starting from home, you are going to need customers. Paid lead sources are a quick way to get you your first customers, but they can cost a lot of money, so be careful and tread lightly. Paid lead sources represent a big category, so we will try to break it down into the basics to get you started.

- Some of the biggest and most well-known sources for paid leads are Google AdWords, Facebook, LinkedIn and Instagram. We would suggest starting with any of these and going slow as you develop your ad content and measure the success.
- You can set up A/B testing within any of the advertising platforms, which will help you compare the ads to see which one is more effective.
- Use video in your advertising, which can be transformative in attracting customers.
- Look for online lead sources that specialize in paid leads for your particular industry and for your business. An example is Bark.
- You can use LinkedIn ads for B2B leads and for attracting potential partnerships.

Please beware that a lot of these advertising platforms are not as user friendly as you would think. We recommend using a well-priced software to navigate these platforms, especially as you get going. Don't invest too much at first and make sure to analyze how the paid lead sources are working for you before investing significant money.

Once you have started to see customers come to you based on the free options that you have used, then consider paid advertising. However, remember that you do not want to pay more for the customer to come to you than what the customer is paying for your services. What paid options can you use?

- You could set up Google Ads to make it where your website is promoted from time to time when people search a certain keyword.
- You can run Facebook advertisements, which are often more affordable.
- Paid-per-click advertising. This protects you from paying for advertisements that aren't reaching your future customers. You only pay every time someone clicks on your advertisement.

Another tool that you have out there are websites that can give you leads in your industry. For example, Bark is a great place to get leads to consumers or business decision-makers who are looking for services that you offer. However, it will cost you so be mindful of the return on investment you get from the sources.

Customer Follow-Up and Satisfaction
In the age of online reviews accessible with every search for your company name, you need to keep your customers satisfied. More than that, you need to make them feel so great about their experience with your company that they're excited to share a great review. Don't be shy to ask satisfied customers to leave

reviews. If you do have an unsatisfied customer, make sure you address the issue right away. If they leave a bad review, address the review publicly to show that you are going to remedy the problem, and then ask the customer to change their review after you have done so. Just a small number of bad reviews will reflect poorly on your business.

Before your customer gets to the review stage, however, you want to ensure that they have a personalized experience. Studies have suggested that a more personalized customer experience is more likely to win customer loyalty and leave them feeling satisfied than a low price point or an excellent product.[2]

Lastly, only make promises you can keep, and make sure you deliver on your promises. A customer will inevitably be disappointed and disgruntled if you have led them to expect one thing and they experience something else. For example, if you have a product where you have guaranteed overnight delivery, and a customer receives it two days later, they will feel that you have broken your promise to them. If you claim your product or service will achieve a specific result or solve a problem, then you need to make sure it does that for your customer or client. If not, you will lose customers and people will be less likely to want to use your business.

Public Relations

Public relations is about hustling to tell your story to those who will give you editorial coverage of your business. You can definitely hire a qualified, excellent public relations professional, but before you do so, you should start with it on your own. Here are some tips:

- **Create a "boiler plate" statement about what you do.** You are going to be asked in the "about" section of every social media platform you set up, so you might as well craft a statement that is persuasive and unique to describe what you do. This statement can also be used in any emails you send to make you sound more professional.

- **Create press releases based on templates that you see.** You don't want to misrepresent who you are, but you can create press releases within Word and PDF that show what you do, based on templates you find online.
- **Send emails to influencers on social and traditional media sources.** Once you have created a boiler plate statement and press release, you can start sending emails to those responsible for news stories and established online audiences. Make the emails concise and establish early on why what you are doing will benefit them and their audience.

A lot of the aspects of your business will flow into your public relations efforts. You can start crafting public relations statements by identifying what inspired you to start your business. Maybe you were laid off during the COVID-19 epidemic and realized that you wanted a more stable income that you control. Maybe you are a new parent who wanted the freedom to stay at home and raise your kids while still providing a service or product. Think of the story you crafted about your business along with your mission, vision and values. You can use this in your public relations work.

The story behind a company is incredibly compelling and can help get you editorial coverage. Where did you get the idea for your company's main product or service? What made you realize this is a product that others may want? You may have designed a new product that makes cleaning your floors easier; perhaps you thought of this after having to mop up another spill from a child or a mess made by the family dog.

These questions start to build the folklore behind your company. Whether you are reaching out to a social influencer to share your story, or even to reporters, there are rules to follow for reaching out. These are not rules that are set in concrete, but they are meant to help you, to ensure that you are not wasting your time on your efforts.

1. Email reporters, influencers and the like on Tuesday, Wednesday or Thursday. This is when they are more likely to look at your pitch and your story. Sending an email on other days decreases your chances of them reading it.
2. Do not reach out to reporters and influencers during the holidays ... it won't get read. Or if it does, people will say after the holidays they will get in touch with you and simply forget.
3. Make sure your email has three solid sections. These sections include (1) a complimentary statement about them; (2) a concise description of your business; (3) what you are asking of them and how it directly benefits them or their audience.
4. Follow up with a phone call a day or two after the email is sent.
5. Track those who have written about your business. You will find that there are several ways of doing this. For example, set up a Google Alert for whenever your business name or your personal name is mentioned. Mention is a tool that tracks mentions on the web and even social media.

Tech blogs are one of the best sources for reaching out, no matter what you are offering. Why? These are blogs that are on the cutting edge and they are usually more than willing to talk about a new product or service, if they believe it will be beneficial to a tech wizard. Likewise, if you are offering something that is geared towards parents, why not contact influencers or bloggers who are often willing to talk about a new product or service if they believe in it. You can do Google searches to find the top blogs that cater to your target audience.

Social Media and Your New Business

One of the best ways to get the word out about your business is social media. Twitter, Facebook, LinkedIn, YouTube and Instagram are just some of the more popular options. An added bonus is that social media is free to use. Social media is a great way to get your brand seen, to get your business name out there, to experiment with messaging to your audience, and to start seeing fairly immediate results.

When people consider doing business with any company, they often look to social media to see how the company is portrayed, looking at reviews and the like. In fact, 54% of people use social media to determine if they should buy a particular product or not, according to studies, and that number will continue to rise.[3] If you are not using social media, you are missing out on potential customers.

For those who are setting up these accounts, it is rather simple to do, as they only require an email address. Be sure that you include your new website in the about sections within all these platforms, as you want to get visitors to your website as well. We will get into more detail in the following chapter but want to offer a few other tips for you to manage your brand on social media:

1. Share information that will give readers an idea of who you are and what you offer. Experiment with posts to see what gets the most engagement as you want to develop a personal relationship with your audience.
2. Enter the conversation. Remember, being on social media doesn't mean that you should be constantly sharing new products or new services that you are offering. You need to share some items that are just for entertainment

purposes. Remember the 80/20 rule: approximately 80 percent of content should be entertaining or educational in nature, while 20 percent should be self-promotional.

3. Start by managing your company's social media yourself. It's an easy and cheap way to experiment with language and imagery to represent what you are doing.

4. Be authentic in everything you post. Remember, you are posting to grab attention, and to develop your reputation. If you are not authentic, people will notice as soon as they see what you are posting.

5. Share items with your logo on them. When sharing products or news related to your services, a custom graphic with your logo goes a long way to help your company. This is something that you can hire someone else to do, such as a freelancer, or even try to do this on your own with graphic design software like Canva.

Email Marketing

Email marketing can help you make specific connections and reach new potential customers. There are several sources that you can use that can send a professional email to contact emails you collect.

For example:

- MailChimp: An affordable solution that will allow you to opt into a free plan for up to 2,000 contacts, then as you grow you can switch to a low-cost solution.

- Emma: An email marketing program that offers custom solutions. What makes Emma stand out is that they have a reputation for amazing customer service, along with numerous templates to make your emails stand out.

- SendInBlue: A free email marketing program that you can use, which they say will remain free for the future. They do have paid options as well that allow for more customization and removal of the SendInBlue logo on the bottom of the emails.

- Constant Contact: A popular email program, but it can be a bit pricey for new businesses.
- MoonMail: A free email marketing plan that allows up to 300 email addresses. It does have restrictions on their free program, but they offer affordable solutions to step up your email marketing game.
- Benchmark: They offer the option to have 2,000 email addresses and send up to 14,000 emails per month on the free plan.
- HubSpot Marketing: They offer a free version that is meant to entice you to their paid version, but it could be a great option for just starting out.
- Omnisend: This email platform is designed for those in sales. They allow you to use their templates, along with sending 15,000 emails per month on their free plan.
- Zoho Campaigns: Their free plan offers 12,000 emails per month for up to 2,000 contacts. From there, they have a pay-as-you-go option for more emails or contacts.

These email software solutions are by no means an exhaustive list. Play around with them to determine which one you like best. You may want to consider which email platform is going to offer better results, better layouts, and is overall easiest for you to use.

The content of these emails can be anything that you want these to be. However, consider these suggestions:

- An email announcing a special sale of your services or products. Making this available to those who have signed up for emails is like giving your audience something special for sticking with you, so it can be an incentive for people to sign up to receive emails in the first place.

- Consider sending something that is all about the local community. This is a great way for those who are doing more business locally. The email can highlight other businesses or even people who are making a difference. It is a great way to gain some goodwill among your audience.
- Showcase any changes that are coming to your business. For example, if you have hired a new person, introduce them via a newsletter so that everyone has a face to go with the name.
- Send an email containing information that prompts them to be interested in what you are selling. For example, if you are running a solar power business, showcasing how solar power saves money can be one way to gain attention.

The sky is the limit as to what you can share. Just make sure that the emails provide value to the reader, whether this is to inform, educate or just entertain. Through the software, you can track and follow up with those opening the emails or signing up for offerings as these would be considered warm leads.

Guest Blogging, Backlinks and More

One of the best ways to start sharing your story and promoting yourself is guest blogging. You can then have a backlink to your website, getting people to come to see you. Guest blogging helps you develop relationships with influencers and helps to establish you as an expert, in addition to getting you great organic search links.

You will want to guest blog on topics that are related to what you are offering in your business. For example, a plumber would write a guest blog on how to avoid clogging your kitchen drains. An entrepreneur who has a new technology product may guest blog on the role of Artificial Intelligence in new programs. You get the idea ... write about what you are offering. This is going to not only help you get your website in front of people, but it helps build your reputation as a professional in the field who knows what they are talking about.

When it comes to backlinks in these guest posts, everywhere you post is going to have different rules on what you can do. Some will allow you to backlink to your website only in the author bio, while others may allow you to hyperlink within the text. You will have to adapt to the individual rules of the website in which you are submitting this content too.

You can start your own blog, but make sure you have a source for content that remains fresh and unique. You can start a blog on Medium, for example. Always be aware of the keywords that you are using in your blogs to allow people to find you in a search. A few other tips:

- Make sure that the content you submit, whether this is a guest blog or an original blog on a site like Medium, is different than what you find everywhere.
- Write in blog format, which means you should have shorter paragraphs with three to five sentences each.
- Break up your text with pictures. You can find websites offering free pictures, such as Splash.com, Pixabay.com, and more.

Another excellent idea is to check out Vocal. This is a newer website in which people can submit opinion pieces, informational how-to pieces, and the like.

There are several other websites that accept guest blogs and can help to build up your reputation. Find websites that are in your niche. Here are a few to consider for your marketing approach:

- Huffington Post
- Lifehacker

- Buzzfeed
- Ehow
- Survey Monkey Blog
- Wise Bread
- Startup Nation
- Women on Business
- Small Business Bonfire

Create a Podcast

You can provide valuable, informative and fun content through a podcast. The advantage to using a podcast to get your name out there is that you can do it in a way that is natural, and doesn't come off like a TV commercial or a radio ad. Use that to your advantage. Be personal and authentic. Appear to inform, instead of selling or convincing someone to choose your company.[4]

If you are a residual income CEO, you might want to have a podcast that covers an eclectic assortment of items related to the properties you run. If you are a gig owner CEO, you can go deep into one area, showing off your knowledge and expertise. You could be interviewed by a podcast creator or start one as part of your business.

Absentee owner CEOs and active owner CEOs can also host a podcast, or have various people on your team do so, to show the relevancy of your business in the marketplace of ideas.

You may think you don't have time to have a podcast, but there are ways you can integrate it into what you are already doing. People tune into podcasts for two main reasons: because they are relatable or because they are offering information. You can show the authentic side of your business, and how much those at your company know through a podcast. You can host interviews with other business owners or experts in your space, or members of your team. You can show what a day as an at-home CEO looks like. A podcast can provide a natural way for people to see what your business is about and it can be a place to show off the products or services of your company. You can also share customer testimonials, by featuring them on the show or a podcast interview.[5]

Another way to use podcasts for your benefit would be to advertise on those that reach your target audience. You could either pay or offer the podcast host an incentive, such as that you would feature their podcast on your website or social media pages in exchange for an advertisement.

The number of people who listen to podcasts has been on the rise, as people want to choose what they listen to, instead of tuning into the radio.[6] Many people who commute to work listen to podcasts, and podcast ads can cost from only $25 to $40 each. If you can find a podcast that is in your space, you should try advertising. Podcasts offer a choice for you in that you can set one up on your own, get editorial coverage on one or multiple podcasts, or you can advertise on them.

Interactive Videos

Interactive video is something you can share on your website, your specific content, or in an email. Interactive video can pause every so often to give the viewer a chance to choose. For example, Maybelline made a tutorial video to show how to use their products, and let the viewer decide which type of makeup style they wanted to see demonstrated. You could also make a video about your company's values, products, or story. There is a lot of room for creativity here, and these types of videos will be far more engaging and effective advertisements.[7]

Share Other People's Content

Sharing other people's content is a way of developing relationships and establishing yourself in your industry. Maybe you're just starting out and your time is filled by setting up your business and making new hires. If so, you might not have the time to create all of your own content for a blog, podcast, or for your website. Instead, remember that it can be powerful to share content that others have already written. Share articles, blogs, quotes from books that you have found helpful, or statistics that you have come across. You don't need to come up with your own fresh material every time. You can share content on your business's LinkedIn and social media pages, too.[8]

Guerrilla Marketing Tactics

Guerrilla marketing is a broad category to capture other marketing tactics that rely on a lot of hustle. You will undoubtedly have many more ideas, as that's part of the fun of growing your audience. Remember that large companies have huge marketing departments but nothing can make up for a dedicated CEO from home, alone or with a team of employees, working to engage and attract new customers with an authentic message.

As you get started, you will most likely cultivate a list of subscribers through your crowdfunding campaign, webpage, social media, beta launch or your network. Don't lose track of them. If they stick around, they can be some of your most loyal customers and can help show off your brand on their own social media channels, website, or through word of mouth. They can also provide ongoing feedback if you make changes to your product, website or services.

Check in with early supporters and customers and ask about their satisfaction with your product and business. Use your email list to conduct surveys, advertise and invite your customers to contests, to give them a tutorial about your service or product, and ask for ways to improve your business.[9] Reply to their concerns, comments, and completed surveys promptly, even if it's with an automated email.

Once you have built up a good customer base and started getting helpful feedback, ask some of those who loved your product, service or business if you can share their review. Post some of the best reviews on your website, your social media pages, and your blog. People sometimes determine whether they will buy something based on a review. Do your due diligence and check out what customers are saying on review websites, such as Google reviews, Yelp, BBB, Angie's List, or others, and make sure you direct your most satisfied customers to post their glowing reviews there. You'll also want to respond to any bad reviews and make sure that you show you are willing to make up for any bad experience. After all, your brand name and business reputation are at stake.

If you have a product, having a contest can be a great way to continually keep it in the public eye. Hold a contest for a cash or product prize where your customers take Instagram photos of themselves using your product. Award the funniest, most creative, or most heart-warming of these. If you don't have a product, a contest can still be a great way to get some cheap publicity. Have a contest about something related to your company or something off the wall and fun that's not related. As long as your business name and an effective hashtag are used, you'll be getting your company out there to potential customers.

You can reward your customers through a loyalty program or exclusive discounts. Try to offer something that doesn't cost you anything monetarily. These gestures will actually make your customers more loyal to you and more likely to refer you to a friend. If a competitor comes along, a loyalty program can be an incentive for your customer to stay with your brand.[10]

People want to know who is in charge of your business. Even if you're camera-shy, be willing to show your face. If people see there is a real person behind the business, and not just an automated system, they are more likely to feel a connection and trust you. As much as possible, try to keep things personal with your customers or clients, talking to them on the phone and always having a picture of yourself in your email and on your website or blog.[11]

Get connected with an organization that is doing good

somewhere. Even if you are only able to make a small donation at first, or are simply educating your customers about the organization that you want them to support, it will show that you care. People are more likely to trust and want to do business with you when you show that you're not just out to make money, but that you also want to give back.

Marketing your business is a process that you will continue to do, even after becoming established. The largest companies out there are posting on social media and sending emails, as they know the value of maintaining their current customer relationships rather than having to find new ones to replace. Have fun with it and get energized with the big wins of attracting new customers.

Chapter 7 Key Takeaways
After reading this chapter, what should you understand?

1. Don't let the marketing objectives for your business derail you from executing on your vision.
2. Take time to pick out your name, and use keywords when you can to make it easier for people to find you.
3. Have your logo showcase who you are and what you do.
4. Don't be afraid to reach out to marketing professionals if you need assistance.
5. Your marketing activities will most likely start with paid lead sources, public relations, social media, email marketing, and guerrilla marketing tactics.

Endnotes
1   Richard Harroch. "12 Tips for Naming Your Startup Business." Accessed October 7, 2020. https://www.forbes.com/sites/allbusiness/2016/10/23/12-tips-for-naming-your-startup-business/#7ca467c7904e
2   Mike Kappel. "Make Your Business Reputation Pack A

Punch With These 4 Tips." Accessed September 6, 2020. https://www.forbes.com/sites/mikekappel/2018/12/17/make-your-business-reputation-pack-a-punch-with-these-4-tips/#4103a1931859

3   Chris Beer. "Social Browsers Engage with Brands." Accessed October 7, 2020. https://blog.globalwebindex.com/chart-of-the-day/social-browsers-brand/

4   George Minton. "Six Ways To Use Vlogs For Business In 2019." Accessed September 3, 2020. https://digitalagencynetwork.com/six-ways-to-use-vlogs-for-business/

5   Dave Hochman. "Want to Advertise Your Business on Podcasts? Here's How to Get Started." Accessed September 3, 2020. https://www.entrepreneur.com/article/349181

6   Eric Siu. "Podcast Advertising: What You Need To Know." September 3, 2020. https://www.singlegrain.com/blog-posts/content-marketing/podcast-advertising-what-you-need-to-know/

7   George Hughes. "Interactive Video: Does it Work and How to Use it?" Accessed September 3, 2020. https://www.smallfilms.com/interactive-video-does-it-work-and-how-to-use-it/

8   Cheryl Baldwin. "LinkedIn Marketing Tips to Grow Your Brand." Accessed September 6, 2020. https://www.wsiworld.com/blog/5-tips-to-grow-your-online-reputation-and-brand-on-linkedin

9   Josh Ledgard. "How to Keep Your Audience Engaged Post Launch." Accessed April 27, 2020. https://kickofflabs.com/blog/how-to-keep-your-audience-engaged-post-launch/

10   Rikke Berg Thomsen. "7 Proven Customer Loyalty Programs That Work." Accessed April 30, 2020. https://sleeknote.com/blog/customer-loyalty-programs

11   "10 Simple Ways To Build A Strong Business Reputation." Accessed September 6, 2020. https://yfsmagazine.com/2017/07/05/10-simple-ways-to-build-a-strong-business-reputation/

Chapter 8

Learn to Sell

As an entrepreneur running a business from home, you will need to learn the ABCs, which is an old but still relevant selling term that stands for Always Be Closing. You will be selling to people to become your client, your employee, and to share their advice for your company. The idea of selling conjures up all kinds of ideas from Gordon Gekko, to *Death of a Salesman,* to nightmares of childhood fundraising, to the last experience you had at a car lot. But anyone can master the art of selling. Whether you offer a service, education, a product, or really anything, you need to attract people with your authenticity and passion to build your business.

One of the most important things to remember when selling is that because of technology, the person you are selling to usually has some knowledge of what you are discussing. Longer ago, selling could potentially involve pulling the wool over someone's eyes, or just being likeable. Now, it's truly about authenticity, the attributes of your product or service, strong communication skills, and following up on what you say you are going to deliver. Regardless of where you are in your journey to feel comfortable selling, we encourage you to let go of any fears you might have and open up to learn.

You may have seen Robert Herjavec on *Shark Tank.* As a successful businessman, he's had to learn how to sell along the way. He shares a few important tips for selling on his website. We'll use those as a jumping off point to discuss how to effectively sell to gain loyal customers and grow your business.[1]

Sell Yourself
People are more likely to buy from someone they know or trust.

Selling bears some resemblance to making a new friend. You can achieve a lot by being relatable, genuine and putting yourself out there. Customers want to know that there's a human being on the other end, who will help them if they have trouble, or who has enough integrity that they're not going to try to trick them.

Tell your customer or client a story. We have talked about the story that you put together for your employees or to send to writers to get editorial coverage. Now share a story that illustrates something about you, whether it's your resilience, your drive, your compassion, your love for people, or your problem-solving abilities.

In the beginning of a client relationship, you can show off your personality while you get to know them. If you're intelligent, don't hide it. You don't want to seem aloof, but if you show people how smart you are, they're more likely to trust your business and your ideas. If you're charismatic, dry-humored, or introverted, let your customers know. Let your customers know you are a person of integrity, who stands by your business and your product or service.

Andre Zafrani, CEO of Apogee, says that he establishes credibility by building and nurturing strong relationships. He is responsive to their needs, reliable and continues to provide quality services, which leads to trusted advisor status.

Listen to Your Customers

Robert Herjavec says, "Good salespeople listen to what their clients are saying. They pay attention to the clients' needs from the start and present accordingly." If you are focusing solely on what you have to offer, and not getting in touch with what your customers actually need or want, then you can talk all day and never make a sale. Customers and clients need to feel heard. If you are not naturally a good listener, you will continue to run into the same walls until you learn how to listen.

No one wants to feel coerced, manipulated, or tricked into buying something. Ask for feedback and let your customers lead the way in terms of how you sell to them.[3] For example, if you say "Ten out of twelve people choose our product over the leading name brand because it is just as effective," that demonstrates that you've put in the time to research and listen to people who would be your customers.

Limit the amount you say in any given pitch, in any situation. Ask questions and share information, then wait for the customer to tell you that they want more information before proceeding. In the meantime, you can ask your customer or client for feedback or to make some kind of decision.[4]

One way that online businesses are listening to and engaging customers in the selling process is through interactive video, which we addressed in our marketing chapter. In fact, as many as 70% of marketers have found interactive video to be a more effective means of engaging customers. Great interactive video is engaging and lets the customer be part of the story. Like a "choose your own adventure" type of book or game, interactive video allows the viewer to make choices along the way that will each take them to a different part of the video. Interactive video does this through a number of ways.

Some interactive video allows the viewer to click on hotspots, which are buttons that will take the viewer to a web page or show them some kind of content. Another interactive method is to offer a 360-degree view, where the viewer can manipulate what they are seeing by clicking, dragging or swiping.

Another popular tool is using branches in the video. At various points, the video will ask a question and then pause to let the viewer click on their response or how they would like to learn more. Then, the viewer will only see content based on their interests. This is a great method for practicing customer listening in the selling process.

You can also use data inputs within interactive video. Every so often, the video will allow the user to put their information in the fields, such as their name, age, or gender. This can be a helpful way to learn about your customers and to keep them engaged and "talking" to you. You could also use a quiz in your video, which combines using buttons and branches. A quiz can deliver a more personalized video at the end.[5]

Selling to your customers and clients needs to include dialoguing with them. You can use open-ended questions to gather feedback, such as, "Why did you choose this product?" Be non-confrontational and let them know you are genuinely interested in what they think and that you simply want to listen.

Personalized Shopping Experience

If you are selling online, you will want to find ways to make the shopping experience more personalized. This can be a challenge, but it is not impossible.

If you are selling some type of clothing, you might want to include a quiz about someone's measurements and provide size recommendations. You should consider providing different sizes and dimensions of your products. You could provide a sizing chart so that the customer feels certain they are choosing the right size for them.

You could use a quiz to help someone find the ideal bike for them, based on how often they will use it, their size, and their activites. You could also do this for shoes, baby products, and a number of other items.

You can check out these apps on Shopify to get you started:

- Kiwi Sizing (kiwisizing.com)
- Visual Quiz Builder (https://apps.shopify.com/product-recommendation-quiz)

You could also make quizzes through these:

- Typeform Quiz Creator (https://www.typeform.com/quizzes/)
- Lead Quizzes (https://www.leadquizzes.com/)

Let's put it this way: the more information you are able to gather about the customer, the more you can personalize their experience. One of the ways you can do this is by recommending products based on purchases they have already made or pages they have viewed.

You can consider using one of the following to help you track customer behavior and follow up:

- Shop Phone, the Shopify App (https://apps.shopify.com/shop-phone)
- Lucky Orange (https://www.luckyorange.com/)
- Listrak (https://www.listrak.com/)

You can use augmented reality to personalize the shopping experience. Augmented reality allows your customers to "try on" your product virtually, or try it out in some way in a virtual environment.

Let's be honest: people want to try things before they buy them.[6] They would probably prefer to touch them, but the next best thing is to see them in a virtual, augmented reality. Augmented reality has accounted for over 50 percent of ecommerce sales in the last several years, and the trend is continuing. Approximately 63 percent of customers feel that augmented reality could improve their shopping experience and 35 percent think that they might shop online more often if they knew this was available to them. One of the most successful ways that businesses have done this is by having a virtual "changing room" where a customer can try items on. Here are a couple of places you can find help to build the virtual reality component of your ecommerce site:

- ZapWorks (https://zap.works), a design suite, enables you to create your augmented reality the way you want. ZapWorks Studio is a more expanded version of this and ZapWorks Designer is the more basic version for beginners. They charge $60 per month if you pay annually.
- Augment (https://www.augment.com) comes already fully designed. All you need to do is add it to your App. Augment is a product previewer that enables shoppers to see your merchandise in a setting such as their home. It does not include features that allow you to try on clothing. The cost is $89 per month.
- Marxent (https://www.marxentlabs.com) is a faster augmented reality option, which uses 3-dimensional images of your merchandise to be displayed, along with 360° product viewing. Their prices vary.[7]

Personalizing Email Campaigns

You shouldn't limit personalizing the customer's experience to shopping. Studies have found that people and businesses are more likely to open an email if it is personalized, such as including their name and the company they work for. However, there is such a thing as over-personalization, which will cost you valuable time and might not drive your click-through rate like you think it will.

The results of some studies suggest that it is enough to personalize the email to address the industry or area of interest to the person. Beyond that, people may see the artificiality of putting personal details about them in the email and it may arouse their suspicion instead of making them more interested. However, it's worth including personal details, such as a potential customer's name, to let them know they're on your radar. The moral of this story is, let your business speak for itself, instead of trying to cater too much to your customer and acting like you are an old friend. It can feel too much like a gimmick.[8]

Know Who Your Customer Is (and Who Isn't)

You aren't selling to everyone. You will want to know who will realistically buy your product or service, and at what price.[9] We've already addressed building a customer persona, or target audience, in chapter three. We encourage you to refer to that to help you determine your ideal customer. The general rule of thumb here is this: whoever is using your product is your customer.[10] This may change along the way.

People who you didn't think would be interested in your product might start buying it, and the demographic you anticipated would be using your product may seem uninterested. If this is the case, you will need to adapt your selling strategy along the way.

Don't make the critical mistake of thinking that you can sell to many different groups who are going to use the product in different ways. This will cause confusion, and will end up as a waste of time and energy. Knowing which groups you are not selling to can be as important as knowing who you are selling to.

Get Inside Your Customers' Heads

Why would your customer want your product in the first place? This can help you think about possible selling points. For example, will your customers come to you because your product or service is inexpensive, or because it is high-quality? What are the main priorities of those who might become your loyal customers? When you're describing your product or service, you'll need to make sure you do so in a way that resonates with your customers. What analogies and anecdotes might appeal to them? Think through the answers to these questions to understand the best appeal.[11]

Gordon Segal, the founder of Crate and Barrel, would tell his floor staff at the store, "You're selling a candlelit dinner by poolside, not a piece of wax on a stick. You're selling romance, not flatware." He believed that success in his stores came from personality and imaginative merchandising; that they were not in the business of distribution, they were in the business of selling.[12]

Work for Your Customer
Know your customer's needs and goals. You need to partner with your customer and put their needs and priorities first. This will help you understand how to reach them and help them feel seen and appreciated for their patronage. Understand your customer's pain point. What is the problem they are trying to solve, or what has gone wrong with another product or service they've used, that's caused them to seek out your business? Focus your sales pitch on them.

Show your customer that you're helping them. Tell them why you care enough to solve their problem. You may be tempted to tell your customer a story something like this: your customer is a damsel in distress, and you are the heroic knight sweeping in to save the day. In short, you end up telling your customer that you're here to rescue them.

Instead of telling this sort of story, however, you need to make your customer the hero. In a well-written story, the hero solves their own problem, with the help of a few wizened spirit guides or sidekicks. You need to paint your customer as the hero who is solving their own problem, with you playing a role in their journey. You need to empower your customers by telling them they can be their own hero and you can help them complete their quest.

Know Your Product or Service and Simplify
If you can't articulate clearly what your product or service is about in a concise manner, it may be a sign that you don't actually know. Get to know your product or service better. Make sure you know it inside and out. Know what you can

guarantee, and any limitations to your product or service. For example, if your service promises quick delivery, make sure you've thought through the particulars of your delivery method and can communicate those to your customers.

You have thought through your business and your product at length. But people are not going to stick around for 20 minutes to read the entire story about your business and how you came to create your product or offer your amazing service. Instead, think about being concise about you and more robust about what they need and how you benefit them.

The Six Stages of Sales

There are six stages to selling into a B2B market. We've adapted those six stages to more generally address selling, no matter who you are selling to. We'll walk you through each stage, briefly highlighting some of the areas to pay particular attention to, as they're where most salespeople lose the customer.

1. Sales inquiry is where initial contact with the customer is established. Here, you want to make sure that you provide the necessary information your customer needs before deciding to make a purchase. This will include all the necessary details about the product or service, such as its features, cost, and benefits. A potential barrier at this point is that the customer might feel you are not fully disclosing all information and might not trust you if you don't explain needed details up front.

2. Needs recognition is the stage where you try to understand the customer's needs better. Make sure the customer already has enough information about your product or service, and ask for feedback about why they need your product or services.

3. Evaluation is the stage when the customer is looking at the product or service you are selling. It is in this stage

that customers might feel that they don't understand the product well enough to make a purchase. It is critical, therefore, to continue to provide ways for them to learn more about your product or service, whether through videos, photos, research, or even a blog.

4. Solution development is when the customer investigates what would happen if they purchased your product or service. In the B2B market, this would mean adopting your product or service into their line. In a business that deals directly with consumers, this would mean the customer is considering how the product might enhance their life. Their mind will go through possible negative outcomes of buying the product, such as that it does not end up enhancing their life or they find that they have wasted their money. To combat these concerns and possible hurdles to a customer making a purchase, companies can offer guarantees, such as short-term refunds if the individual or business doesn't like the product.

5. Decision is simply when the customer makes a final decision to buy your product or service. Customers will focus on risk in this stage, too. Make sure you are aware of the risks you are asking your customer to face, and address those in this stage to alleviate their concerns.

6. After-sale maintenance takes place after the sale has been made. To avoid losing money, or getting bad reviews, you'll want to follow up with your customer in this stage and make sure they're satisfied. If they aren't satisfied, address the issues quickly. A happy customer is more likely to become a loyal customer.[13]

Pronoun Help: Use "You"

Studies by Corporate Visions have shown that using "you" in your phrasing throughout your content and communication is much more effective at drawing others in and helping them to feel that they should take some kind of action.

As you start selling, be mindful of common hurdles. For example, you should know how much time you will have to invest. New products will take more time to sell, whether it's a new product you've invented in your line, or your brand is offering a competing product with another brand. For example, salespeople spend an average of 32 percent more time interacting with customers over new products than with existing ones.

The status quo bias is your customer's bias to continue with the behavior or item they have been using, rather than trying something new. It is much harder to convince someone, for example, to switch to your service or product if they are already using something similar or feel they have already found a solution to their problem – even if yours is better than what they are using.

People naturally find comfort in maintaining the status quo. They shop at the same stores and habitually buy the same products, because making endless decisions about everything takes time, energy and research. Therefore, you need to communicate to them the urgency to change. They might see your product or service and be interested, but they won't be motivated enough to make a change unless they can see why they need to do so immediately. Chances are, if you aren't convincing enough to make them take immediate action, they are going to forget about your product, service or business.

To help you combat the status quo bias, you'll need to make your pitch unique. You need to show your customer that you understand and can meet all of their needs, especially ones that other brands aren't picking up on.[14] For example, if you are running a food delivery service, you can promise convenience. You can promise quick delivery times. But what about the quality of the app on their phone? Are there issues or pain points that most other brands don't pick up on that you can tap into? If your message sounds the same as all of your competitors, you may become lost in the mix and lose business due to the status quo bias.

Once you gain a customer, however, you will want to use the status quo bias to your advantage. Show them the continued value you are adding to their life and thank them for being your loyal customer.

The Successful Salesperson

The successful salesperson is the one who spends more time on selling new products and services, and less time on existing ones. This person will pare down and target only customers who they think will actually be interested in buying the product or service. In short, they are focused.

To be successful, you also need to keep long-term goals in mind. Think about slowly building a trusting relationship with your customers and clients, instead of simply focusing on getting them to buy something from you right now. Building a trusting relationship with your potential customers has been proven to be a far more effective strategy.

Think about the barriers to making a successful sale and focus on overcoming those. You need to be concerned about the purchasing process and how your customers are making their decisions as much as you are about the actual product and how it is being presented.

Don't sweat the small stuff. It's easy to get discouraged when you don't see immediate sales or there are setbacks in the selling process. All those little details won't determine your success, however. Instead, your determination to press on and to solve each problem that comes your way will aid you.

Always be willing to learn. Don't ever think you know all there is to know about selling. Pay attention to what works and what doesn't. This will help safeguard you against making the same mistakes, and will help you to face challenges more readily. Also, you'll want to gather as much information on the front end when you're selling a new product. It might drag down your performance at the beginning, but it will pay off in the long term. You will find a better way of selling, ultimately.

Sales requires a lot of adaptability. You will need to change your strategy at times and account for new variables that you didn't anticipate. Don't stubbornly stick with your strategy when new information suggests that it is ineffective, or has hit some kind of roadblock.

Additionally, the successful salesperson is humble. Being humble means you have a realistic idea of your abilities. One study found that salespeople tend to rate themselves high across the board, in every category. Their customers, on the other hand, rated them as knowing a lot about their product, but being deficient in other areas, such as adaptability. Sometimes what you will need as a salesperson is honest feedback from your customers about how they perceive your performance.[15]

Answering Objections

Inevitably you are going to hear a no. Even worse, you might hear a maybe or something that you think is a yes that evolves slowly and painfully into a no. Here are tips to identify and answer objections to close a sale:[16]

- Address the objection. Empathize and agree with the barrier.
- Identify the true issue. Be sure to drill down into what the true issue is for the objection.
- Break down and solve. Once you understand the true objection, you can break it down and solve for a sale.
- Provide proof and react to signals. Give proof of what you are selling through third-party, credible independent sources that will establish trust and move you through the objection.

B2B selling is somewhat of a different animal than selling directly to consumers. The stakes are usually higher, and you will use some different methods to sell to them. Many of the principles we have discussed in this chapter will be the same, however. One tip we have specifically for B2B selling is to show the company what they will lose if they don't go with you. According to Prospect Theory, people are more likely to base a decision on avoiding an unwanted outcome versus taking a risk to receive a gain.[17]

Build a Great Ecommerce Page

Selling also happens passively through the ways you have represented your business online. To create a great ecommerce page, make sure it is clearly and stylishly laid out. Display your products in a way that captures your customer's attention and shows them all their options.

You can capture your customer's attention by announcing or featuring items on clearance, or where your customer can save money. Don't be afraid to use a little humor, too. Displaying clever product names, taglines, or descriptions can capture your customer's attention.

Make sure your pages are well designed and concisely inform your customer about your products or services. Take a look at some ecommerce pages that draw your eye and take notes about what they've done. You can get some great ideas this way.[18]

Other Places to Sell Ecommerce Products

The second-best thing to having a storefront window on the main street or being in a prime location in a shopping complex is being in a prime location on the Internet. You may be thinking that you need to design your own ecommerce presence for every product you offer, but that's not the case. There are many places people regularly go to shop online, where you may want to strategically sell for your business.

The first, and most obvious of these, is Amazon. They will charge you a number of fees, so you'll want to price your items accordingly. For example, the individual selling plan will cost you $0.99 per item you sell, as well as a referral fee. The professional selling plan costs $39.99 a month, but you don't pay per item you sell.

A good reason to use Amazon is because of its popularity. You are likely to draw in customers who wouldn't have connected with your brand another way. If your product is more unique you can get more attention faster. If your product is a common one, such as socks, then it may get lost in the thousands of other people selling socks on Amazon. Over time, you can earn reviews to get your socks to rank higher in a search, but in the short term, this might not be the best way to make an initial splash in the market.

Another place you can consider for an ecommerce product is eBay. Though it is less popular than Amazon, it is still a major online shopping place. You could also potentially earn more money on your merchandise, if people want your product and start trying to outbid each other. The cost to you will be around 10% of the price you sell an item for. Additionally, if you hit 50 sales per month, eBay will start charging you $0.30 per listing. EBay has options to pay more to promote your merchandise. To set a reserve price, which is the lowest price someone can bid on your product, you will have to pay a fee as well. EBay can also be effective if you have merchandise that is rare, valuable or you want to see how much someone will pay for it.

Next, you might want to consider Bonanza. Bonanza is similar to Amazon and eBay in its eclectic collection of what is sold. There are various fees, based on the price of your item and its shipping costs. Bonanza will help you to advertise across the Internet for additional fees.

If you want to keep your sales local, you might want to try Craigslist, Facebook Marketplace, Virtual Garage Sales, or

Letgo (which is now partnered with OfferUp). You'll need to do more of your own marketing and outreach if you take one of these routes, but you'll get to keep more of your profits. These also often involve meeting up with the person you're selling to.

For selling clothing, vintage items, or crafts, you should think about using one of these:

- Poshmark is a great place to sell clothing and other items. Sales under $15 will cost you $2.95, and sales above $15 will cost you a 20% fee. The buyer will pay for the shipping, which simplifies matters.
- Ruby Lane is primarily a place to sell vintage items. You can post as many as 50 items for a $54 maintenance fee each month. If you have more than that, you'll have to pay a little more. Additionally, there is a 6.7% fee on a customer purchase.
- Etsy allows you to sell crafts, art pieces, or vintage items. You'll pay $0.20 to list an item and then a 5% fee once a sale is made. There are additional fees for using their payment system.
- The RealReal markets high-end used clothing and articles.

If you're selling electronics, you might want to check out one of these places:

- Swappa
- Glyde
- Gazelle

These sites will give you a quote. Then, all you have to do to get paid is send the electronics to them and they will pay you for your item and resell it.[19]

You will not only be the CEO for your business but its chief salesperson. Selling is critical for nearly every aspect of what you will be doing with your business. Don't be afraid to jump right in and start. Beginner's luck can be very effective if you work hard to establish it and then to develop your sales technique as you go.

Chapter 8 Key Takeaways

After reading this chapter, what should you understand?

1. Sell Yourself. Be relatable, authentic, and a person of integrity. You represent your brand.
2. Learn to listen to your customers. Ask for their input and feedback in the selling process and take it to heart.
3. Know who you are selling to, and who you are not.
4. Understand and work for your customer.
5. Know your product or service inside out and be able to explain it simply.
6. Think long-term about building a trusting relationship with your customers when you're selling.
7. Personalize correspondence and the selling process.
8. Use augmented reality in the shopping experience if you have a visual product.
9. Build a great ecommerce page or find the best place to sell online for your business.

Endnotes

1   Robert Herjavec. "My 5 Essential Tips for Selling Anything to Anyone." Accessed September 15, 2020. https://www.robertherjavec.com/5-essential-tips-selling/

2   Brian Tracy. "How To Sell Anything To Anyone In 2020." Accessed September 15, 2020. https://www.briantracy.com/blog/sales-success/how-to-sell-anything-to-anyone/

3   Steve Tobak. "How to Sell Anything to Anybody." Accessed September 15, 2020. https://www.inc.com/steve-tobak/how-

to-sell-anything-to-anybody.html
4   Tony Parinello. "How to Sell in 60 Seconds." Accessed September 15, 2020. https://www.entrepreneur.com/article/65972
5   "What is Interactive Video?" Accessed September 16, 2020. https://www.wyzowl.com/what-is-interactive-video/
6   Dayna Winter. "A Perfect Fit: 7 Ways Brands Use Personalization to Create Tailor-Made Shopping Experiences." Accessed September 15, 2020. https://www.shopify.com/blog/personalized-shopping-experiences
7   Matt Ellis. "Augmented Reality for Ecommerce: Complete Guide for Online Stores." https://www.ecomdash.com/augmented-reality-in-ecommerce/
8   Tim Riesterer. "20 selling techniques that will actually improve how you sell." Accessed September 15, 2020. https://corporatevisions.com/selling-techniques/
9   Robert Herjavec. "My 5 Essential Tips for Selling Anything to Anyone." Accessed September 15, 2020. https://www.robertherjavec.com/5-essential-tips-selling/
10 "Accelerate Revenue Growth by Defining Customers Differently." Accessed September 18, 2020. https://strategyn.com/outcome-driven-innovation-process/who-is-your-customer/
11 Steve Tobak. "How to Sell Anything to Anybody." Accessed September 15, 2020. https://www.inc.com/steve-tobak/how-to-sell-anything-to-anybody.html
12 "10 Great Entrepreneurs Talk About Their Startup Days." Accessed October 7, 2020. https://www.inc.com/ss/10-great-entrepreneurs-talk-about-their-start-days
13 Thomas Steenburgh and Michael Ahearne. "How to Sell New Products." Accessed September 15, 2020. https://hbr.org/2018/11/how-to-sell-new-products
14 Tim Riesterer. "20 selling techniques that will actually improve how you sell." Accessed September 15, 2020.

https://corporatevisions.com/selling-techniques/

15   Thomas Steenburgh and Michael Ahearne. "How to Sell New Products." Accessed September 15, 2020. https://hbr.org/2018/11/how-to-sell-new-products

16   Ira Kalb. "How to be Great at Selling Even if You Hate It." Accessed October 7, 2020. https://www.businessinsider.com/the-secret-to-greater-success-is-learning-how-to-sell-2013-10

17   Tim Riesterer. "20 selling techniques that will actually improve how you sell." Accessed September 15, 2020. https://corporatevisions.com/selling-techniques/

18   Courtney Symons. "15 Drool-Worthy Product Page Examples to Inspire Your Own Ecommerce Store." Accessed September 15, 2020. https://www.shopify.com/blog/product-page

19   Stephen Layton, Laura McMullen. "8 Places to Sell Stuff Online." Accessed September 15, 2020. https://www.nerdwallet.com/article/finance/where-to-sell-stuff-online

Chapter 9

Learn the Administrative Side

Running a business involves creativity, strategy, and team building. But it also involves the administrative side. Unless your business is all about administrative duties for other businesses, chances are you may be dreading this part of the job. However, it is a necessity for any CEO, especially one wearing so many hats in the beginning.

There will be one-time, semi-frequent and regular administrative duties with your business. If you are not particularly attuned to these you can definitely outsource them. But these tasks are usually fairly quick and painless and you will want to stay lean in the beginning by doing as much as you can on your own to avoid unnecessary costs.

One-Time Administrative Duties

The one-time administrative duties may be one of the least exciting parts of setting up your business, but they are some of the most important. Most of these steps can be done in very little time, especially if you are a small business and you plan to be an LLC. These include creating the necessary articles of organization or incorporation, getting your tax identification number, and filing for any business licenses you need.

This Articles of Organization is simpler than the Articles of Incorporation. You will file for this with your Secretary of State if you are becoming an LLC. You will answer the same kinds of questions and go through the same steps as identified under Articles of Incorporation above.

Next come the bylaws. Instead of coming up with bylaws, as you would for a larger corporation, you may create an LLC operating agreement. As this is a smaller business, you may need to register it annually or biannually, depending on your state's regulations.[1] Bylaws in the beginning can be incredibly simple. They can also be more complex and are the rules that will dictate what your shareholders, directors, and officers will do. If you have a lawyer, they can help you prepare these. The bylaws will be put into effect by the board of directors. They will stipulate the following types of items:

- The number of directors on the board
- The timetable and mode in which board and shareholder meetings will be held
- Tasks to be performed by directors or officers
- Voting procedures and regulations
- Stock transference regulations
- Legal protection of the officers, directors, and shareholders
- The corporation's fiscal year duration
- General information about dealing with corporate matters

Since you aren't a big corporation, you don't need a stock ledger. Instead, make sure you have a list of the names and addresses of LLC members and what their holdings look like. Keep track of any transferred units, dating each transaction.[2]

If you are in the U.S., you will file for a tax ID number, which is simple. Go to the IRS website, and then file the paperwork. It takes minutes to get this and is free. Watch out for scam websites that charge you a fee for this service.

Next, you will want to set up a merchant account and credit card with a bank. You need a way to collect the money that you are owed for your products or services. Setting up a merchant account can be done in several ways. You can opt to do this through PayPal, which is a trusted service that many businesses use. You may even be able to set up a merchant account through your bank. Stripe is also a great source for getting recurring payments. You can apply for a business credit card through various sources, similar to a personal credit card.

You need some form of accounting software to look at what you are spending and how much you are making. Intuit QuickBooks, for small businesses is a great option, and is affordable. However, you may find that a free software will work as well, depending on your needs. For example, Wave Accounting is a free option that can link to your merchant account.

Depending on which industry your business is in, and your state's regulations, you may need to set up a business license. There are different regulations based on where you live, too. You may need to get one of the following types of business licenses:

- A general business license – Your business may need this license. You will need to look up how to get this in the city your business is in.
- A professional/occupational license – Some business industries, in certain states, will require this license. Some of these occupations include lawyers, accountants, or child care businesses.
- A state license – You need a state license in some states if you are serving alcohol. Some states require a state license to show you follow certain state regulations which pertain to your business.
- A federal license or permit – You may need a federal license or permit if your business has anything to do with an area that is regulated by the federal government, such as pertaining to alcohol, firearms, fishing, and wildlife.[3]

If you do not get a business license, it could end up costing you down the road. Your business could face legal ramifications for damages or could receive penalties. Your company would not be protected by the local, state, and federal laws. You could be fined or shut down, and you could be personally held liable. For all of these reasons, make sure you obtain the proper licenses and you check if your business needs any special permits.[4]

The Articles of Incorporation, also called Certificate of Incorporation, are a two to three-page document you will create and submit to become an official C or S corporation. You will need these only if you are a larger corporation. If you want to keep things simple, as we recommend, then you will file to become an LLC.

Here are the steps for the Articles of Incorporation:

1. Select a corporate name. Choose this carefully, as this will be the legal name of your business going forward. Make sure that no one else already has the same name. You can pick out an entity name with the state and then a DBA "doing business as" and specify the business name that exists online or in another format, but if you can keep it simple from the beginning it is best.

2. Select a state of incorporation. We recommend you become an LLC, as this is more affordable.

3. File an official document with the Secretary of State. You can google the website, download the form and send it in. You can also call to ask questions from the business services group of the secretary of state. You can also use a lawyer or go through an online service such as LegalZoom or Rocket Lawyer.

The Articles of Incorporation should include the following:

- The name of your corporation or business.
- Why you want to become a corporation. This could be because you want to engage in business in a legal manner.
- Duration. LLCs typically have a duration of twenty

years or less. You usually don't want this duration to be indefinite.

- The authorized capital. Here, you'll quantify the value of your shares, classes of your stock (if applicable), and the number of shares your corporation can issue. Make sure you include the founder's shares, as well as any that might be given to employees or investors.
- The name and address of your agent. You need to have a registered agent, who will handle any lawsuits against your company in the future.
- Look at your state laws. There may be other items that are required to be included.

You can find many types of forms and helps in this process at: https://www.allbusiness.com/forms-agreements. There are some other documents you may need to create as well, depending on the size and structure of your business.

The Action of Incorporator is a document, made by the incorporator, who is the person who originally organizes the corporation. This could be a lawyer, a shareholder, or some other individual. This document is used to adopt bylaws, elect directors, and sign the Article of Incorporation. If your Articles of Incorporation don't name the corporation's board of directors, you need to create this document and make sure to date it after the date that you are officially incorporated.

The Buy-Sell Agreement allows the corporation to buy and sell stock. Sometimes shareholders want to or need to withdraw, and their stock will need to be bought. You will need to set the price of the interest in buying and selling arrangements.

This agreement will also help to regulate the following:

- In the case that the corporation needs to dissolve
- A partner or spouse's consent to buy/sell, should the shareholder be unable to make the decision

- Repurchasing options for the shareholders
- What types of transfers are permitted

If you need to create a buy-sell agreement, then you should consider using a lawyer.[5]

Semi-Frequent Administrative Duties

There are some tasks you will need to perform more frequently. You will annually check if you need to update your articles of organization or incorporation. If an update is necessary, you'll need to file the articles of amendment. You will need to file the articles of amendment when you are changing the name of your business, or if you need to register a change in the membership ownership, a change in name or address of your registered agent, a change in the financial structure of your business, or a change in mailing or principal address of your business.

There are several other small operating changes which may or may not require you to update the articles. You will need to look up the laws for your state on the SBA.

Your business bylaws should spell out the process to get the changes approved. After you have gone through the approval process with your business, you will need to fill out government forms to change the articles of organization or incorporation. Lastly, you will need to file these articles of amendment with the proper state agency and pay any fees.[6]

You will have monthly and quarterly payments to make, too. You will need to pay income tax on a quarterly basis, no matter what type of business you are, if you expect to owe income tax of $1,000 or more. If you have employees, you will need to deposit the federal income tax that is withheld from your employees, along with federal unemployment taxes and social security and medicare taxes for both yourself and your employees. These deposits can be made monthly or semi-weekly.[7]

You may also need to pay sales tax if your company is in a

state that requires it. Check the SBA to determine what kinds of taxes your business should be paying.[8]

You will also need to review the payroll process quarterly and make any outstanding payments. You may have a payroll service that creates and files these reports.[9] A good tip is to use a firm like Paro to hire a bookkeeper to help you keep track of the accounting pieces of your business. You can use your bookkeeper, combined with QuickBooks, and a check-in by your accountant to make sure you are following all of the rules.

Chances are, most services you subscribe to for your business will have annual subscriptions you need to review and renew. You may need to check the invoices and renew your subscriptions for the following:

- Your website/domain
- Email services
- Scheduling Apps
- G Suite
- Microsoft 365
- Any software subscriptions or payment services

If you are not administratively gifted and you don't want to risk missing a payment and having an important service cancelled, you can usually set up automatic annual payments.[10]

You will also need to update your privacy and terms policies on your website on a semi-regular basis. You need to make sure that your privacy policy accurately details the following:

- Any personal information you collect from your users, such as their names, addresses, telephone numbers, or email addresses.
- What your company collects the information for: is it for analyzing how they are using the website, for communication or shipping purposes, or to follow up

with them?

- Any cookies your website uses and why. Usually cookies are used to increase the website's functionality.
- Any third parties you need to share their information with for analytics or maintenance purposes.

You'll want to assure your customers that their privacy matters to you and tell them the security measures you have in place. However, you will want to warn your customers about malicious malware that you cannot protect them from, and encourage them to protect any information they give to the site so that someone can't access it.[11]

You should consult with a lawyer before drafting your initial privacy statements, and consult that lawyer any time you need to update your policies.

Regular Administrative Duties

There are regular administrative duties involved with running your business. Here is a list to get you started:

- Recording every transaction and possibly using an accounting software such as QuickBooks.
- Documenting and filing receipts and invoices. Create a system to keep these organized, such as filing them alphabetically.
- Reviewing any outstanding payments you need to make to vendors or other parties. Stay on top of all of your IOUs and make payments as quickly as possible.
- Sending invoices and receipts to collect payments from your customers.
- Reviewing and tracking your cashflow.[12]
- Creating a payroll system and schedule. You can either have an inexpensive service do this for you, such as Intuit Payroll, OnPay, or Gusto,[13] or you can create your own

system that can keep track of employee hours, wages, deductions and withholdings, and direct deposit.[14]

- Using QuickBooks or some other financial help to create and keep your budget. Spreadsheets will only get you so far when it comes to business expenses.
- Keeping track of key performance indicators, or KPIs.

Staying Lean During the First Two Years

After we have explained all of these administrative duties, it is important to talk about staying lean for the first two years. So, how can you do this?

1. Avoid any unnecessary fees such as working with a lawyer, accountant, PR professional or the like. While you may need some people like this eventually, you are better off trying to do this yourself at first. However, for accounting purposes like paying quarterly taxes, consider freelance accountants and bookkeepers through a company like Paro. If you have used QuickBooks, then the person only needs to run some figures; it may only take two to four hours. If you can get someone at a low rate, then it may pay you to do this.

2. If your business needs equipment, try to find good, used options when starting. You can always upgrade later. For example, if you are starting your own T-shirt printing business, check out eBay for used printers to get started. Often, by buying used you can save 50% or so on the final cost.

3. Delay a physical office for as long as possible, if not indefinitely. Too many people make the mistake thinking that their business is going to be so successful they need to rent a building or they need to build on a room of their home to accommodate this growth. Do as much as you can from home in the environment you have now, then

look at these options later, and only if your business has grown to this extent. After all, you are setting out to run a business from home; stick to this goal and enjoy not having to pay the rent on an office.

4.   Consider using open source software to make it cheaper to run your business. Tons of software out there is free to use since it is designed within the open-source community. It may be lacking in some things, but the free part of this is going to be appealing during your first two years.

5.   Keep a close eye on your expenses and cut these when you can. For example, maybe you are paying for an email marketing program that sends out 2,000 emails per day. If you are only sending 300 per month, then look elsewhere.

6.   If you need help, consider outsourcing to freelancers. They are often much more affordable than hiring someone full time to work for you.

7.   Need office supplies like pens, paper, printer ink, etc? Then shop during the back to school season and stock up for the rest of the year. This can be a way to save 20 percent or more on the items that you will be using throughout the year.

These are just a few examples of how you can cut expenses and stay lean during your first two years of business. After the two years, you should have a better idea of what you are earning, what you are spending and the potential that your business has so that you can grow in the best way possible.

Free Open Source Resources

When we talk about the administrative side, you can often save time by using software, but the cost can easily add up. For this reason, open source programs can be a great option. Here is a list of some sources that you could use for your business administrative needs:

- GNUCash: This is recommended for both personal and small businesses and it can be used across several platforms including Linux.
- Openmiracle accounting software: It can prepare financial reports, profit/loss, and several other features. And it is completely free; it is often the direct competitor of GNUCash.
- LibreOffice Writer: A great alternative to avoid having to pay for Microsoft Office.
- Google Docs: Completely free to use for word documents with a Gmail account.
- OpenSourceBilling: A software that allows you to create and send invoices to clients, that includes partial payment tracking.
- Logic Invoice: A free self-hosted accounting and invoicing software, considered one of the best open sources on the market.

This is just a partial list of what you can find in the open source market. Do some research to see if the software that you need is available in an open source format; you may be surprised at just what you can find.

Not many people set out to start, acquire or continue to run a business from home and get excited about the administrative side. But the administrative side of any business is nonetheless important and it is worthwhile to explore shortcuts to get the job done.

Chapter 9 Key Takeaways

After reading this chapter, what should you understand?

1. You can set up your business on your own without the additional legal fees that so many people think about when they hear a business startup.
2. Be as lean as possible during your first two years to ensure the survival of your business.
3. Use free software out there to make your job easier. There are free programs as options that can help you stay lean.

Endnotes

1 Jean Murray. "How to File Articles of Organization for an LLC." Accessed September 7, 2020. https://www.thebalancesmb.com/how-to-file-articles-of-organization-for-an-llc-397776

2 Richard Harroch. "10 Key Issues in Setting Up an LLC." Accessed September 5, 2020. https://www.allbusiness.com/10-key-issues-setting-llc-110074-1.html

3 Belle Wong. "Starting a Business: License and Permit Checklist." Accessed September 7, 2020. https://www.legalzoom.com/articles/starting-a-business-license-and-permit-checklist

4 HBS. "Do I Need a Business License for My Company?" Accessed September 7, 2020. https://www.delawareinc.com/blog/do-i-need-a-business-license-business-license-info/

5 Richard Harroch. "An Overview for Incorporating a Business." Accessed September 5, 2020. https://www.allbusiness.com/overview-incorporating-a-business-103646-1.html

6 David Gass. "How to Update Articles of Organization." Accessed September 28, 2020. https://andersonadvisors.

com/how-to-update-articles-of-organization/

7   Georgia McIntyre. "The Complete Guide to Filing and Paying Small Business Taxes." Accessed September 28, 2020. https://www.fundera.com/blog/small-business-taxes

8   Kristin Ewald. "Business accounting: 21 steps to tackling this like a boss." Accessed September 28, 2020. https://quickbooks.intuit.com/r/bookkeeping/small-business-accounting-checklist-10-things/

9   "Checking your billing subscriptions." Accessed September 28, 2020. https://support.squarespace.com/hc/en-us/articles/115015286787-Checking-your-billing-subscriptions

10   "Checking your billing subscriptions." Accessed September 28, 2020. https://support.squarespace.com/hc/en-us/articles/115015286787-Checking-your-billing-subscriptions

11   J. Gerard Legagneur, Esq. "What to Include in Your Website's Privacy Policy." Accessed September 28, 2020. https://www.nolo.com/legal-encyclopedia/what-to-include-in-your-website-s-privacy-policy.html

12   Kristin Ewald. "Business accounting: 21 steps to tackling this like a boss." Accessed September 28, 2020. https://quickbooks.intuit.com/r/bookkeeping/small-business-accounting-checklist-10-things/

13   Jared Hecht. "The 5 Best Payroll Options for Small Businesses." Accessed September 28, 2020. https://www.entrepreneur.com/article/285855

14   Matt D'Angelo. "How to Do Payroll." Accessed September 28, 2020. https://www.business.com/articles/how-to-do-payroll/

Chapter 10

Build Your Online Presence

When you are ready to start your new business, people will need to find you online. We have discussed your marketing strategy, which will inevitably include your online presence, but we want to go into it with more detail here. You might have other marketing tactics, such as direct mail or traditional advertising, but the cheapest, easiest, and most ubiquitous way of reaching customers is online, so we want to focus on it here. We will break down your online presence into the following categories: websites, search engine optimization (SEO) and social media.

Website Design: What You Need to Know

You can definitely get away with just doing a Facebook or Instagram page at first, but your website will be important as a central hub of information in addition to lending credibility. Your website is a way for people to get in touch with you, to connect with you through social media, to read the latest content that you post (such as a blog or introducing a new product/ service), and it can be one of the best ways to start making a visual brand of yourself.

Websites are important, but take your time in spending the money and resources on developing a website. According to eCommerce Foundation, 88% of consumers will research a product, service or brand online before they make a purchase. What happens when people cannot find anything about you online? They lose trust in whatever is being offered, and they look elsewhere. For those who are selling a product or service, this means you just lost a potential customer.

There are also vital design elements that go into making a functional website. Did you know that 48 percent of people polled stated they would not do business with someone if the website was not appealing or was too crowded? According to Blue Corona, not only are 48 percent of people leaving if the website is not that great, but you only have 10 to 20 seconds to win them over as this is when they form their first impression of your business.

The importance of your website cannot be overstated. And to know what you need to do, you should consider the mistakes that are commonly made in website design.

Mistakes New CEOs and Business Owners Make with Website Design

When you are looking at the website of a new business, there are some commonly found mistakes, which can be avoided. Here are a few of them:

1. Your website takes too long to load.

   In most cases, people are expecting a page to load in two seconds. If it takes longer than this, they are not waiting. Instead, they are backing out and going to a different website. Why is your website loading slowly? This could be due to having too many graphics on the page or it could also be an issue with the server. In other situations, having too much flash work on a website can cause it to load slower as well as having html code that is not clean. Remember, it is essential to have a fast upload time.

2. Contact information is not easily found.

   People need to be able to find you quickly and easily. If there is not a face, a physical location or even phone number associated with your website, most people immediately think it's a scam. You will want to have a contact page or section set up that includes your company's email address, phone number and even social media pages in which they can get in touch with you and ensure that you are in fact, a "real" person. Even better, you can include a picture of yourself and your team.

3.   The website only works on a computer.

The idea of having a website that only works on a computer is the equivalent of simply not caring. And this is what customers are going to think when they try to bring up your website on their mobile device and notice that it does not fit. This is where 'responsive design' comes into play, so it incorporates multiple devices.

4.   Too much or too little content.

There is a fine line to walk when it comes to the content that you put on your website. Sometimes a business website fails to establish the company's dominance in the field. Even if you are new to the industry that you have chosen, you have to make your content look like you are the chosen professional. The customer wants someone who says, "I'm the professional in providing you with marketing services ... I have years of experience that can be put to work for you." Be sure to break up the content on your website to make it easy for readers to go where they need to answer their questions. Make your website's content easy to read on multiple devices. Follow the guidelines of only using a few sentences per paragraph, breaking up large blocks of text for graphics, and the like.

5.   The graphics are underwhelming or overwhelming.

You are going to want to use the graphics on your website to help make you more trustworthy and appealing. For example, those who are designing clothes often put pictures of the clothes that they are offering on their website to give an idea of what they offer. However, the key is to find the right mix of written content and graphics. Remember, too many graphics can slow down the speed at which the page loads to the device. However, you do need to use graphics on your website to help break up the written content.

6.   There is no SEO on the website.

This is a mistake that new business owners as well as established business owners frequently make. SEO is crucial to your website so you can appear in organic searches. However, you want to be sure your website appeals to real people and not just the bots that are perusing your website to appeal to algorithms.

Be sure to evaluate your website as a detached, active web user. Ask friends and family to check it out as well to collect feedback. You will quickly have your website going in the right direction.

Elements Your Website Needs

While there are several elements in website design, one phrase that will continuously pop up is responsive design. What does this mean? Responsive design allows your website to work with different devices. A website that only looks good on a computer is obsolete, as there is so much search through phones and tablets. Responsiveness is becoming a no-brainer whether you decide to make the website on your own or to hire a professional.

With this being said, there are other essential elements for your website. These include:

1.   Identify the goals of your website

What are you hoping to do with the website? Are you using the website to continuously showcase new products? Or will it be the hub for your personal brand? Knowing your goals will help you make the elements of your website work well together.

2.   Make your website simple and easy to navigate

No one should ever come to a website and not see a clear layout of where to find the contact section. A good rule of thumb is that with every page that a person navigates they should never be more than two clicks away from the homepage.

3. Focus on your home page

Remember, this is the first impression that you are making on those who visit your website. The goal is to leave a positive impression within 10 seconds of the person seeing your website. Make sure the logo is prominent, the colors are pleasing, and the navigation is on point.

4. Create a clear call to action

You want your website to have a clear call to action. You might have a button that simply says, "Have a question, contact us" or it could be "Learn more about our service, click here." You might offer a freemium model so someone can try your service for free for 14 days. Whatever the call to action, it needs to be seen and be engaging enough to result in people actually taking the hoped-for action. Remember, this is vital to ensure that every person who visits your website has the potential to be turned into a conversion.

5. Quality, unique content is key

It is not enough to have a website that looks good, it also needs content that is informative and gives a clear idea of who you are and what you are offering. You need to have content that will engage those who visit the website. When the content is high quality, readers are going to trust you more and it can lead to more business leads. You may find it helpful to set up a blog on the website so that you can share quality content this way. What can you share? For example, a CEO starting a company offering online counseling sessions might offer content about how counseling is essential and how it can be done online or over Zoom.

6. Make a Frequently Asked Questions page

   People often search for answers to questions. Make a "Frequently Asked Questions" page that offers answers not just about your product, but about related questions people might type into Google. For example, one of your FAQs could be, "Do I need a life coach?" with a response that covers the benefits of having one. It might bring a customer to your page and, when they're there, it can convince them to consider using your business.

7. Make your website mobile-friendly

   The reality is that most people who are viewing your site will be doing so on their mobile devices. As that's the case, you'll want to make sure all your pages are readable and rank just as highly on mobile devices. You'll want to use Shopify or a mobile-friendly test such as the one by Google (https://search.google.com/test/mobile-friendly) to make sure it works okay.[1]

8. Don't overthink the privacy and terms statement on your website

   You may or may not need a privacy and terms statement on your website but we encourage you not to overthink this step in the beginning. We suggest that you check out privacy and terms statements that are related to your business and make the first draft on your own and then have an attorney friend read over the statements on your behalf, rather than paying money to have someone craft them from scratch.

Everything that you do for your website is meant to boost your business. As a CEO from home, your virtual business base online will reinforce the credibility and integrity of your company. If your website is poorly constructed, it is going to be a direct impression on you, the business owner. The need for a visually appealing and content-rich website cannot be overstated.

Designing Your Website: DIY or Use Professionals

You have the choice to build your website on your own or use a professional team. We have talked about the money and time trade-off, and you will need to make a decision on your available resources in terms of creating your website.

To build a website on your own, you can use a website builder like Wix or WordPress. These building tools have wizards to get the website where you want it to be, and you may spend very little money to use these tools. If you have the patience and time, you can probably teach yourself to do the fancy themes that you see online, or at least find a plugin that is going to give you the same effect.

If you craft the website on your own be sure to show it to family and friends and get their first impressions. Did they feel like it stood out? Does it remind them of another website? Do they like its visual appeal? Remember, the average person will make a decision on whether they like a website within the first 10 seconds of seeing it. You can also set up some test advertising in order to see how the website will be received. You can easily spend $100 towards Google AdWords or even on Facebook advertising to steer people to your website. Be sure to set up Google Analytics to see what people are doing on your website and how they interact with it. This can be a good way to see if the website is a hit or a dud.

You can hire a group of back-end software developers to craft your website and put together the front end on your own. You would develop what is called a wire frame for your website, which is a basic drawing of each page on the website. Wire frames are easy enough to make with the right software. You can use PowerPoint on a basic level. Another choice is Balsamiq. The specialized software can be as little as $90 for a project, making it a cheap investment compared to hiring front-end developers.

If you are not that technical or simply do not want to spend the time diving into the DIY website building tools out there, you could always hire a professional website builder to do the work for you. Many people feel that this allows you to get a professional website up and running in less time and with better results. A professional website builder offers benefits, including the following:

- They will do the work, and usually faster since this is what they do for a living.
- They can take your ideas and run with them, using the right type of technology to get the results that you want.
- You still have creative control in terms of font choices and colors if you want, or you can leave this up to them.
- In most cases, SEO is already included in building your website, so that is one less worry that you have to contend with.
- Your website developer might also offer virtual IT support to you and your growing company.

You will most likely spend a minimum of $5,000 with a firm for a website that has fairly basic pages. If you are developing a specialized software as the basis for your business you could easily spend anywhere from $100,000 to $500,000 and beyond.

Remember that your website will have these major aspects: graphic design, content, user interface and front-end development, SEO, and back-end development. You can use a website like Crowdspring to help develop the graphic design of the website. Crowdspring is full of freelance artists who will put together beautiful designs for your website. You can also consider hiring freelancers through Upwork to help develop your content, as well as SEO. You will need a lot of user interface and front-end development if you have a complex online offering. For most, though, you will either turn to a website company or tools on your own to do your back-end development of the website.

Getting Your Website Up and Running

Whether you decide to design the website on your own or hire a professional, you are going to need to set up a domain and then focus on the SEO of the website.

Your domain is going to need hosting in order to be seen. There are a few options to consider, including:

- GoDaddy
- HostGator
- Bluehost
- Hostinger
- DreamHost
- NameCheap

If you are looking for hosting, be sure to check out their up-time guarantee, how easy it is to use, what type of support they offer, and if they offer a guarantee. Remember, some of these hosting sites are going to offer a free domain name purchase or it could be designed to work even better with WordPress. Do your homework and find the one that best fits your needs and budget.

An SEO Primer

What is SEO? SEO stands for Search Engine Optimization. It is the way in which Google ranks your website when certain keywords are googled. It helps your website to be found when people search for terms related to what you are offering to your customers.

SEO Refresher

Your goal in using SEO is to rank higher in relevant searches for your product, service, or company. For example, if you type in your business name, what appears in the list of Google results? Even though your new business name is an exact match for your query, your website won't rank very high unless you add details to the search. You will need to build credibility over time, before Google's algorithm decides your website and business are legitimate.

Keywords Are Key

One of the most well-known components of SEO are keywords. Google AdWords has a great keyword planner for you to use. It can help you get some keyword ideas and see how many people search those keywords on a monthly basis. It is free to create an account and use this search component. SEO Metriks is an app that allows you to monitor and analyze your SEO. They have their own keyword program, too, which you will have access to if you pay a low monthly fee for their app.[2]

You can insert frequently searched keywords in your website content, but you can also use them to tell you what kind of content you should create. For example, if you searched for your business type and name, "Life coach consulting coached to success," and found "Wooden's pyramid" and "pyramid of success" were related, highly searched keywords, you might want to include a page on your website or blog with a title that includes those keywords and describes what it is and how it relates to your business.

Optimize the Pages on Your Website

You can really slip down a rabbit hole with SEO and your website ranking. Be mindful to optimize your pages, or hire someone to do it, but don't go overboard. Establishing your website is a marathon, not a sprint. We want to put together some very basic thoughts on SEO for your website.

In terms of SEO tags, you should only use an H1 tag once on

your page, ideally on the title, and include your top keywords. Keep in mind that you want your page title to be short enough so that it is easily understood when it appears in a search engine, 50–60 characters at most. Make sure that the title still makes sense to a reader, as using too many keywords can garble the message. For example, using the page example from above, your title might be, "Using Wooden's Pyramid of Success in Life Coaching."

You'll want to make the most of your meta descriptions, too. Meta descriptions are the short descriptions that appear under the title of your page when it is displayed in Google search results. They should be attention-grabbing, with a call to action, and have under 155 characters. For example, "Wooden's pyramid provides the key to success. Learn about how you can apply it to your life today."

Additionally, while you may not have been able to afford a more expensive, competitive URL in the formative stages of your company, once you get going you can invest in a URL that includes one of your most highly searched keywords. This can enhance your search engine rankings.

Finally, take one last look through your website. If you have any images, video or audio content on your website or blog, you will want to make sure you tag them with keywords.

Here are a few tips for your SEO:

1. The website address, or domain name, should have some form of your company name in it, plus it can even have some geo-targeted information as well. A great example, if you are starting a business to offer career coaching for those in the Long Island area, you may find that the domain name www.careercoachinglongisland. com would be effective.

2. Be sure that the domain name is not something so long that it can't be remembered. Remember, a shorter

domain name is better in terms of the quick attention span consumers have when searching online.

3. SEO should be included within the title of your website pages. The title of the page is meant to tell the search engines what the page is about. For example, if your business will be offering digital marketing services and you are trying to target "digital marketing" as the keyword, then a title on one page may be "10 Ways to Use Digital Marketing." The title is going to not only help you appear in searches for digital marketing but also help search engines to see that you are legitimately offering this type of advice, helping you to rank higher.

4. Be sure that your meta descriptions have your keywords in them. The meta description is going to provide a summary of the page in 190 characters or less. And you need to make sure that the keyword you are trying to rank for is included in these.

5. Be careful about the keyword density throughout your website. With the above example of digital marketing, you don't want to have the phrase appear too many times. While search engines are not as particular about this as they were in the past thanks to the Natural Language Processing they are using, your website will be ranked lower if they feel that the keyword density is too high. This means that if you are putting "digital marketing" into random places on a web page that makes no sense or using this too much in general, it is going to cost you.

Don't become overwhelmed with SEO. In fact, with a WordPress site, there are plugin options that allow you to monitor SEO. It will allow you to see when SEO needs work on a page or blog post. For example, if you add a blog post you will know if your target keyword is good in your content, title, and even meta descriptions. If you feel like you are not doing well enough with SEO, you can always hire a professional freelancer later to go through and audit your SEO to make sure that you are following the rules.

Social Media

We started out with some basics about social media in the previous chapter but let's roll up our shirtsleeves and get into more detail here. Social media is great because you can cheaply and easily develop content for your brand. We would highly recommend getting it started on your own. It won't take a lot of time at first and it will help you establish ideas around how you want to represent your company. You can hire a social media service to take over in time, but start it on your own to develop an idea of what you need.

You will want to select one or more social media platforms for your business. Next you will want to develop content for your social media presence, including imagery and hashtags. Finally you will want to cultivate, build, and most importantly maintain your audience. This is an overly simplified start in social media but let's jump in.

First, you want to decide which platforms are right for your business. Start by thinking about the essence of what you're doing. Does your business lend itself to being quirky, visual, or serious? Do you need to connect with consumers or business decision-makers? What are the demographics of the people you are selling to?

The landscape of social media is constantly changing, so we can't summarize all the platforms, but can offer an overview of what we believe to be the most relevant social media platforms for your business:[3]

- Facebook: Great for most companies. One of the most popular and established social media platforms, but is trending toward an older audience. Encompasses video, visuals, news, networking and entertainment. Customers can easily reach out to you and interact with your brand.

- Twitter: Ideal for most serious, news and research-focused companies. Twitter can offer trending hashtags and it's easy to retweet a post or tag someone in a post to interact with them.
- Instagram: Perfect for companies that want a sophisticated, visual focus. Instagram is a visual medium that incorporates pictures, graphics and videos that are mainly focused on entertainment. Instagram particularly appeals to young women and moms.
- YouTube: Great for further explaining what you do through video. You can easily make a short video focused on entertainment or education and post it within a channel dedicated to your company. We recommend keeping most videos to a minute and a half or less and cross promoting these videos.
- LinkedIn: Great for businesses focused on getting leads from other companies (B2B) and developing partnerships. LinkedIn covers news and business-related networking, and is mainly filled with text-heavy posts with some graphics and pictures.
- Pinterest: Ideal for platforms that are very image-focused with a hobbyist audience. Pinterest is a general interest platform focused on pictures and graphics in the entertainment sphere. We wouldn't highly recommend Pinterest as we have found it's harder for the average small business to use this platform for marketing, unless they are highly visual.
- Nextdoor: Great for hyperlocal businesses. It's still an emerging social media platform from a marketing standpoint (not a user standpoint) that is text-heavy and focused on news and networking within specific neighborhoods.

- TikTok: Ideal for targeting a young audience. TikTok is incredibly addictive and people spend a lot of time on it. It's still considered an emerging social media platform that encompasses mobile phone-created video used for networking and entertainment. TikTok users could be moving to Reels because of security concerns, but we will see where the momentum leads.

Once you have selected one or more social media platforms you will start developing content. What do you want to say that isn't generic Internet content? How do you stay authentic to what you're doing? We recommend developing a social media editorial calendar to map out the things you are going to talk about and when you want to discuss them. Here are questions to ask to develop your content:

- What makes your company special?
- What topics are going on around the proverbial water coolers that you frequent?
- What is the essence of your company's story?
- What do you want potential customers to know about what you offer?
- What motivates you to serve your customers?
- What are non-controversial things that we all have in common? (e.g., holidays, current events)

Remember developing your story to hire people, attract investors, and find people to give your new company coverage? That story can now be used to attract customers through social media.

In addition to the words in your content you want to think about your images. You will want to use the logo you've created and think about the type of look you want for your business. Do you want an ultra-modern look with stark, white backgrounds in your images? Would you like a look that conjures up more homey feelings? Or are you looking for bright colors to attract someone to what you offer? These are some of the questions you will want to ask yourself as you start to experiment with how you represent the imagery of your company. Luckily, you can edit things easily in social media and experiment to see how engaged your audience is based on what you post.

Here are some ideas for your imagery:[4]

1. Get inspired. Find images online that you like and figure out why you like them. Is it the graphics, the logo, the colors, the images?

2. Use a font that's easy to read. You can stay with the basics like Arial, Helvetica, and Times New Roman or expand to something unique to your company. Just be sure to use the same font family for every graphic you make.

3. Incorporate your logo. If you are going to the work to post a picture to social media, you should try to incorporate your logo. You can put it discreetly in a corner or center it at the top. You don't need to put your logo on everything, but on things that could be shared or reposted, you'll want to make a cohesive link to your company.

4. Be aware of the design size. Different social media platforms call for different sizes. While you can use a general image size of 800 x 800 pixels, which usually works with most platforms, your visuals will have more of an impact when you use the ideal size for the right platform. Here are some pointers:
    *   Instagram: 1080 x 1080 pixels
    *   Facebook: 940 x 788 pixels
    *   Pinterest: 735 x 1102 pixels
    *   Twitter: 1024 x 512 pixels

5. Keep your design clean. Don't overload your design with all the tools, elements and colors that are out there. A good tip is to keep your design to two or three colors that are complementary, in the same shade, or in the same color family.

After these ideas for images, you'll want to select some hashtags. Hashtags are easy to use, change, and create a fun story for your company. You can divide hashtags into specific ideas for your business such as #salesboxersells or #salesboxersocial. Then you can use hashtags that are specific to a product or service that you offer. Next, if you are in a specific location, tag that spot. Finally, you can use hashtags that are trending and more general to what you are doing. Check out Instagram or Twitter to find popular trending hashtags and, if your posts are related, use those in addition to hashtags that are more specific to you.

Now, it's all about cultivating, growing, and maintaining your audience. The Internet is a big wide world in which your company can get lost. Be sure to put out authentic content so you can forge ahead with a loyal group of followers for your audience. Our tips?

- Get to know your audience. As you have started to gather feedback for your company or your idea, you can figure out who is most interested in what you are selling. Get to know everything about them: where they go online, what they do, and their demographics.
- Make it fun for your audience to follow you. Most of the time, for most companies, it really works to make it fun. You can post an Instagram Story that is off-the-cuff, you can put a quiz question on Facebook, and you can post a random thought on Twitter. Being original and fun is not usually a bad thing on social media.
- Find shortcuts to your audience. Think about your

audience and actively look for shortcuts to find them. This might be through partnerships with like-minded companies or through influencers on social media that can refer their audience to you.

- Measure feedback from your audience. There are insight tools within the social media platforms that can help you measure engagement with your audience. Use these tools to actively engage with and grow your audience.

Stay Active on Social Media

It should be a given that those social media accounts you set up should be used. Once you establish your accounts, be sure to not forget about them and maintain contact with your followers. The social media platforms could be your greatest ally in continuing to spread the word about your new business. You may even consider expanding your social media presence at this point, if it's sustainable. You can consider hiring a social media company to develop content for your audience.

Also don't be afraid to use your LinkedIn page to post updates about how your business is developing. People love to hear a business success story and it can help spread awareness and excitement about your work.

Thank people for mentioning you or sharing your posts on their page. Keep track of keywords that seem to draw people to your brand (they may not be the ones you've been using). Show that you're an authority in your area of business by posting informative, helpful posts. Engage, engage, engage. If people start commenting or asking questions, you need to have someone to engage them. Comment or like some of their posts, too. Hire or assign a person on your team to be your social media guru if you haven't yet.[5]

Through your website, SEO tools, and social media, you can establish a very credible presence for your new company. Your online presence is essential to all the other tools that will help you grow faster and create success for you as a CEO from home.

Chapter 10 Key Takeaways

After reading this chapter, what should you understand?

1. Decide whether to build a website on your own or hire a professional.
2. Understand the dos and don'ts of your website design.
3. Know the importance of SEO, but don't spend too much time or money on it.
4. Establish an authentic social media presence for your new company.

Endnotes

1   Samantha Renee. "What Can I Do to Help My Store Rank in Search Engines?" Accessed April 27, 2020. https://www.shopify.com/blog/seo-checklist-online-store

2   Samantha Renee. "What Can I Do to Help My Store Rank in Search Engines?" Accessed April 27, 2020. https://www.shopify.com/blog/seo-checklist-online-store

3   Chambers, Morehead, Sallee. Make Your Business Social. Business Expert Press, 2020.

4   Chambers, Morehead, Sallee. Make Your Business Social. Business Expert Press, 2020.

5   Josh Ledgard. "How to Keep Your Audience Engaged Post Launch." Accessed April 27, 2020. https://kickofflabs.com/blog/how-to-keep-your-audience-engaged-post-launch/

Chapter 11

Be Efficient and Credible at Home

Imagine waking up, doing a quick workout, and heading into your office down the hall after getting the kids off to school. Forget all about the long commute times and uncomfortable wardrobe. Sound like a dream? As much as reality can be so, working from home is pretty great. Working from home presents a long list of benefits including an oftentimes better balance between work and life, much needed flexibility, and a lighter carbon footprint for the environment.

As with all things, there are drawbacks. The challenges of working from home include not always being your most efficient, feeling like you aren't as credible compared to colleagues in an office setting, and missing out on in-person adult interaction. There are strategies to follow to make sure you experience more of the benefits than the drawbacks.

Many people were forced to work from home during the COVID pandemic. Some people hated being away from the energy of the office. Most people, though, were pleasantly surprised at how easy it was to work from home. The *New York Times* referenced a Gallup survey that found a majority of Americans working from home would continue doing so "as much as possible" after the pandemic.[1] Employers opened their eyes to the possibilities of working from home. Let's walk through ways to counteract any potential drawbacks, including being more efficient as a CEO from home, more credible, and supplementing your adult in-person interaction.

Manage the Little Things at Home

You can easily make small changes to enhance your efficiency at home. We've put together a list and while they are really common sense, and you've seen them before, we want to be sure to do a comprehensive review because these little things add up. The larger changes come more from changing habits and are therefore a bit more complex to alter, so let's start with the smaller, easier things.

- **Enhance your work space.** You need a space that is clutter-free, non-distracting, and has all the materials you need. Does this sound too idealistic? Maybe you're starting out working in your bedroom, or at the kitchen table. Wherever you work, try to create a special space that is just for your work. Make rules and boundaries with your family about the space, telling them that they can't come into it and interrupt you because it is your office.

- **Consider the temperature and the air.** Can you adjust the thermostat in your workspace? Many studies have proven that if the environment is too cold, it can make you feel sad and unproductive. If temperatures are too hot, however, it can make you cranky. Figure out the perfect temperature for you. Most people find 65–70 degrees Fahrenheit to be the best for them.[2] Maybe open a window or have a fan going for a little air movement in the room. Sitting in a stuffy room where the air isn't moving can make you drowsy.

- **Invest in the proper equipment.** A standing desk helps keep you alert and in a healthier position compared to sitting all day. Even better, get a walking pad to put under your desk so you get your steps in. A good office chair can save you from back, neck, and other muscular tension problems down the road. Experiment and figure out how you work best. Experiment with the lighting: do you focus better with natural light or a bright, overhead lamp? Or, maybe you need a lighting scenario that can be adjusted to fit your mood.[3] You will want to make sure your lighting and video setup works to your advantage when you are on Zoom calls. Get an ergonomic keyboard and mouse if you need to do a lot of typing, scrolling, and clicking. Use noise-cancelling headphones to block out the noise from your environment. Even if you aren't a person who is easily distracted, it takes extra energy to block out distractions and to help your mind stay on task. Some of these things are simply helpers that will save you some mental and emotional energy as you attempt to focus and get things done quickly.

- **Dress for your job, even if you're working from home.**[4] Sure, it might feel more comfortable to lounge in your PJs, but putting on your work clothes will help you take your work more seriously and professionally. You can think of it as putting on your professional self, and then you can take it off again at the end of the day, when you're done working. Getting into a more professional look doesn't need to include an uncomfortable suit and tie. After all, Steve Jobs was known for his black turtleneck and jeans. Find something that marries style, function, and your brand, and helps get you in the work mode.

- **Stay mentally alert by eating healthy at home.** Planning your meals and snacks at the beginning of the week will save you time and help you to eat more intentionally. Choose healthy foods, in moderate quantities. Eating too much, or eating too many fats and sugars can make you feel sluggish and sleepy. To be more efficient, eat some great brain foods such as fresh fruits and vegetables, almonds, eggs, avocados, and lean proteins such as chicken. Figure out which foods energize you, and avoid ones that make you bloated, gassy, crampy, or tired. Your diet can impact your mental alertness and health, which will directly affect how efficient you are able to be.

- **Get outside and exercise.** Take advantage of the time

you're saving working from home by getting outside whenever you get the chance. You can take walking meetings if you're on a phone call and don't need to be chained to your desk. One study done by the American Psychological Association showed that people are more productive on days that they are able to get physical activity before their work.[5] If you're not a morning exerciser, don't worry. You can still experience an increase in mental alertness and efficiency the next day if you exercise in the afternoon.

- **Keep good posture.** Some companies have become aware of how bad posture can lead to a decrease in efficiency and productivity, and have started giving their employees posture trainers to wear at work. One study found that as many as 85 percent of these workers became more aware of their posture, and were able to correct bad habits that were making them tired or causing distracting pain.[6] Some common posture problems you may have could include craning your neck, slumping, crossing your legs, or curving your spine in unhealthy ways. You should try to get the ergonomic tools that you can, but then once you have them, you need to do the work to learn how to have correct posture. If you practice correct posture, you will keep yourself out of the chiropractor's office and will feel less pain and tension in your body. You will need to spend less time trying to care for your body, because you are being proactive. While you are working, you will notice more mental clarity.[7]
- **Make sure to get good sleep.** A report put out by the CDC found that one third of Americans do not get enough sleep on a regular basis. The problem with this is that it leads to an increase in health problems, such as an increased risk for diabetes, high blood pressure, and an overall increase in mental distress.[8] In addition, a study done by Harvard

University found that employees often miss work and are less productive due to sleep deprivation.[9]

Manage Your Time at Home

Your time is always important, but it becomes essential when running a business from home. Some have joked that their spouse, roommates, children, or pets become their new coworkers. Just like your coworkers can distract you by sharing the latest gossip, or making loud noises in the next cubicle over, whoever you share your space with will provide distractions and may want to get your attention several times a day. Set aside times that are okay for family members or pets to be noisy or have your undivided attention, and then communicate to them the times of day when you will need space and quiet to get your work done.

A study performed by Florida State University discovered that having 90-minute blocks of uninterrupted work time will lead to increased focus and productivity.[10] Guard your time and your space so that you can make the productive work happen.

You also need to have boundaries with team members. Let them know your work hours so that they know when they can contact you, and when they can't. You're not a machine and it's not healthy to be on all the time. You can be more efficient in the time you give yourself if you limit your work hours and availability each day. It also helps your team set healthy boundaries for themselves.

- Make friends and family members aware of your work hours, so that they don't call you or stop by your house during your crucial work time. Don't make appointments during your work hours. Try to schedule them during your downtime.
- Don't check your text messages, unless you use your

phone for work and are expecting work-related text messages or calls.

- Don't check or respond to personal emails all day long. Set aside specific times to check your emails.
- Don't go on Facebook or social media, unless what you are doing there is work-related, such as posting on your business's account.[11] One study discovered that most Americans spend 15 to 18 hours each month on Facebook.[12] Think about how much time and energy you could be channeling towards your work or life instead.
- Write down what you need to do each day and make sure it gets done. Don't make your to-do list too overwhelming, or you might lose motivation. Try to pare it down to the bare essentials. What must get done today, no matter what? What would it be nice to get done? Then, add a third tier of small tasks to do when you're in-between other, larger tasks. You can sandwich a smaller task in that transitional stage, so that you feel better when it gets done and it can motivate you to continue moving forward.
- Try a zero-based calendar. This concept suggests that every minute of your day should be budgeted and given a purpose. It helps you keep yourself accountable for the time you are spending on various activities, whether work-related, personal, or self-care. The zero-based calendar method will help you to block out your work time and exactly what will happen during those hours, so that you make sure everything gets done. You can also block out events and special family time, to make sure that work does not override those priorities. Having less open-ended free time will actually make you more efficient and productive.

Enhance Your Habits

We've all fallen into the trap of trying to do many things at once. We get overwhelmed with the amount of things we have to do, or feel torn between the things we want to do and the things we should do, so we try to do it all. The end result is that we are less efficient. Studies reported by the American Psychological Association have shown that multitasking is particularly inefficient when we are trying to do tasks that have multiple components or steps to them, or are something that we are still learning how to do.[13] This is because it takes time and mental energy every time we switch our attention from one thing to another. If you are watching TV while sending out emails, you are losing precious time and brain power every time you look at the TV and then try to refocus on sending an email. Or, if you're a parent, you lose time and energy every time you speak to your child in the middle of getting your work done.

Your business doing well depends on you doing well. Don't burn yourself out. If you're losing steam, motivation, and focus, you may need to take a quick walk to clear your head, do 15 minutes of yoga in the middle of the day, or take a quick lunch break with your family. Taking breaks can help recharge you so that when you return to your work you will be more clear-headed and efficient.

Also, don't let yourself get too stressed out. If your mind is always on work, then ironically you will be less productive, as you will be building up more stress in your body and then will feel depleted when you're actually doing the work.

One study found that a vast number of people miss work each day due to stress. You will inevitably have stressful times when you are less efficient and effective. What you can do, however, is to try to do things to reduce your stress, which will overall boost your efficiency and make you less likely to be forced to take a day off down the road at what could be a critical juncture.

One of the advantages of working from home is that you can

control the environment and the variables a little more. But if you simply try to do as much work as possible each day, without prioritizing, eliminating or delegating unnecessary tasks, then you will burn out and will be less productive.

Timothy Ferriss, the author of *The 4-Hour Workweek*, puts it this way:[14]

> Effectiveness is doing the things that get you closer to your goals. Efficiency is performing a given task (whether important or not) in the most economical manner possible. Being efficient without regard for effectiveness is the default mode of the universe.

Ferriss is emphasizing that it is far better to be effective than to be efficient, at least in terms of how people seem to view efficiency in the workplace. In his chapter on effectiveness, Ferriss discusses Pareto's law, which posits that 80 percent of outputs result from 20 percent of inputs. He suggests that, to be more productive and effective, we should focus on the 20 percent of the things we think we need to do, which are going to yield the 80 percent of our outputs.

Instead of thinking about efficiency as doing as much as possible in as short a time period as possible, Ferriss argues that, "being busy is a form of laziness – lazy thinking and indiscriminate action. Being overwhelmed is often as unproductive as doing nothing, and is far more unpleasant. Being selective – doing less – is the path of the productive."

Here are some questions to ask to make yourself more productive each day.

1. If you only had two hours to work each day, what things would you absolutely have to do?
2. If you had to eliminate 80 percent of the things that you

are doing (some of them you could ask someone else to do), what would those be?

3. What tasks would you want to pay someone else to do? Which ones could an assistant do for you?

4. Are there things on your to-do list that might not produce any results, or will produce very little even if the intended result comes to fruition?

5. What kinds of things do you do just to feel productive? Do you pay attention to whether those things are yielding the desired result?

To be more effective and efficient, you'll need someone to delegate some of the 80 percent of the tasks that you don't have to do personally. Instead of creating endless spreadsheets, composing and sending emails, and doing data entry and analysis type tasks, you can hire a virtual assistant.

The advantages of working virtually and hiring virtually are discussed in the chapter on hiring good people. Additionally, there are some specific sites you can use to hire a virtual assistant, such as Zirtual (https://www.zirtual.com/). At Zirtual, a company has trained people to be virtual assistants. You pay a monthly fee for a plan, starting at $449 a month for 12 hours of work, if you're not sure that you'll need an assistant long-term. You can use a website like this one if you don't have time to go through the whole hiring process.

Some of the specific advantages of hiring a virtual assistant are that you can spend more time focusing on your areas of strength. Chances are, you are a visionary or manager type. You want to focus more on big picture items and motivating and leading your team. A virtual assistant can help you not to get burned out or hung up on the small stuff.

Think about a part of your business that has to get done, but you struggle to do it because of a lack of time, energy, motivation, or skill. This could be an area that you outsource to a virtual assistant.

There are two main types of virtual assistants. These include:

- The General Virtual Assistant – This person performs routine, daily, repetitive tasks such as emails, scheduling, data entry, quick research, or monitoring and posting to social media. You need to assign them specific tasks to do at certain times.
- The Specialized Virtual Assistant – This assistant has specific skills and can oversee a specialized area of your business. These areas may include bookkeeping, project management, graphic design, creating or editing video content, etc. You'll want to give these specialists an end goal and then let them use their experience and expertise to accomplish it.[15]

Connect with Your Team from Home

It's important at home to both have adult interaction and cultivate a community for your team, especially when everyone is working remotely. In the beginning, if you're starting a business, you will be doing this on your own. In time, or if you purchase a business, you can assign the task of chief community creator to someone on your team.

First you will want to create a remote culture statement. This can easily feed into your mission statement but it's a strategy and an idea for everyone in the organization to follow. Talk about the benefits of working remotely and all of the values and interests that the team shares. You can also outline basic rules for working from home. You can pick a cause as a team that you want the business to contribute to and talk openly about why it's important to each of you. Your established mission statement can also feed into this overall contribution and sense of purpose.

Next, you will want to make sure you are touching base

with team members in a personal way. You can do this through Google Hangouts, Microsoft Teams, or Zoom, or if you're local, taking a coworker for lunch. Check in and make sure that team members are also doing this. The engagement of your team will help you communicate more effectively and helps for employee retention. You can add a mentorship or buddy program as well.

Finally, you want to make sure you are bonding consistently with your team. You might want to set up an events calendar. In terms of bonding specifics, you can do lots of games such as virtual trivia or ice breakers. You can also do a weekly lunch, book club and virtual birthday parties as ways to connect with your team and make sure that everyone is engaged. You can use all sorts of software to make group projects for your team go more smoothly. Some of the platforms and tools you should consider using include:

1. Zoom — Use this for videoconferencing. You can have team meetings or share your screen with your employees to make communication easier.

2. Slack — Use this for communicating information. This is an alternative to keeping track of emails. Instead, Slack offers channels where you can see all conversations pertaining to a specific project in one place. You can have real-time conversations, or see the conversations others are having about the project in real time. Additionally, it is connected with Google Drive, Dropbox, and a number of other tools that you can integrate.

3. Basecamp — This is a project management tool, which allows you to keep track of tasks in to-do lists, and check them off when they're done. You can keep track of the progress of different types of projects, use the message boards, and share important scheduling items. They offer a business plan for a $99 per month flat fee, which includes an unlimited number of projects and users. You

may want to use this plan if you are a residual income or gig owner CEO and have many different users you are communicating and sharing files with.

4. Trello — Trello also uses message boards and lists. It is a tool to help teams prioritize tasks and easily keep track of items the team has already accomplished. Trello has several different plans it offers. You can try it out using their free plan, which includes unlimited personal boards, cards, and lists, as well as up to 10MB per file attachment. If you're working on bigger projects that you want to share with others, and you want to use some of their other features, such as App integrations and automations, then you may want to use their business plan for $9.99 per month.

5. Confluence — Use this for getting templates and for a number of different projects, and easily sharing those with your team. You can share announcements and ideas, and get feedback instantly. You can use it to streamline information to spread knowledge across the board. Confluence's free plan includes some of their basic features, for up to 10 users. At their standard, $10 per month plan, you can have up to 10,000 users and use some of their more advanced features, such as App integrations, archives, and page insights.

6. Miro — Use this for collaborating with your team. You can use it to run meetings and workshops, brainstorm with your team, get aligned with stakeholders, create boards for specific projects, use unique visual maps and diagrams to trace complex processes and systems, and strategize and plan. They have free plans for unlimited team members that include using their premade templated, core integrations, and basic attention management. For more advanced access, you'll need to pay $8–$10 per member per month.

7. Google Suite — This is helpful to use for the options that Google Drive provides. You can share spreadsheets, Google docs, a team calendar, and use Google Meet or Hangouts. Many of these can be used for free, as long as your team members each create a Google account. However, for $6 per month per team member, you can use their Currents feature to engage employees, their Sites to build your website, and Apps Script to automate and integrate.

8. Dropbox — This allows you to share many different kinds of documents in various capacities, across different devices. This is not a communication tool, but is rather more focused on file-sharing. Their basic plan, which includes storing up to 2GB, is free. Their plus plan offers features such as mobile offline folders and content and accident protection, for just $9.99 a month.

Be Credible from Home

In addition to efficiency in your home office, there are many subtle and indirect ways that you can establish credibility working from home. The most important element to remember, from the very beginning, is confidence. When you are confident about what you know and how you have set up your business, it comes through loud and clear. The location from where you are working shouldn't matter. Next, you will want to establish overall professionalism in every aspect that an interested party in your business could see. This confidence and professionalism comes through to establish your overall credibility.

There are a lot of ideas for establishing professionalism in your office and your business.

- Establish a solid personal LinkedIn presence. Whether you are new to LinkedIn or have been part of the platform for eight years, make sure you have listed every professional accomplishment and represented yourself in the best light.

- Create a strong personal LinkedIn, online, and social media presence. We have discussed this in our section on online presence, but be sure to showcase your company in the best way possible where anyone could find it online.
- Put together a personal bio and resume. Make sure your bio and resume provide the right details to represent you in the best way and match your LinkedIn presence.
- Make sure your personal social media presence is on brand with what you are doing. Your clients will end up being some of your social media followers; it just happens. Make sure you are on brand and professional with how you represent your personal life and weekday work habits.
- Make sure your email, email signature, and voicemail greeting are all professional. You will want to set up an email address that caters to your business and ideally has your company name in the address. You will want your name, email address, and phone number prominently displayed in your email signature. You will also want to make sure your voicemail greeting represents you in the best light.

Next, we are going to go through the ways you can specifically develop credibility with your employees, vendors, clients, and your board.

First, you'll want to develop credibility with your team by:

- Not tolerating low performance from your team.
- Using daily huddles among the management team to touch base and ensure strong communication.
- Being transparent about how your business is doing.[16]
- Proving your competency to analyze and solve problems.

- Being dependable.
- Being consistent in the messages you are sending out and the tasks you assign.
- Being authentic. Share your areas of strength and weakness with your team.
- Being honest in your communication. Don't pretend you're okay with something when you're not. Learn to be direct and stick to what you have said.
- Communicating with respect to your employees. Don't simply order them around.
- Admitting when you made a mistake and showing that you can fix it.
- Being loyal to your employees and not throwing them under the bus when something goes wrong.
- Sticking to your principles. Show your employees that you have character.[17]
- Creating opportunities for your employees to socially interact.
- Building rapport with every member on your team and getting to know them personally.
- Using video to communicate as much as possible. Virtual communication is limited and you can miss important nonverbal cues.
- Having one-on-ones once a week with each of your employees to check in on them.
- Helping your employees develop in a way that will meet their career goals.
- Using gifs or emoticons when communicating with employees to help convey emotion.
- Getting together with your team once a year in person if possible.[18]
- Managing everyone's expectations. Have regular check-ins to make sure you are all on the same page about the work you are doing and the deadlines.

- Focusing on the outcome of your employees' activity. Don't push them to work more, but encourage them to meet the desired outcomes or goals of their work regularly.
- Making sure everyone on your team has the resources they need.[19]

Next, make sure you build credibility with your vendors by having clear communication and a security plan in place for transactions:

- Ask your vendors about their cyber security, and let them know the protocols and safeguards you have in place to manage your own.
- Get to know your vendor by doing research on them.
- Have a point person you are in regular contact with.
- Let your vendor get to know you, your team, and your company.
- Develop policies and a contract for working with each vendor. Communicate these policies to the vendor and have them agree to the contract.
- Meet with someone from your vendor in person or on a video call.
- Use multifactor authentication, including Radio Frequency Identification (RFID) cards or biometrics.[20]

In building credibility with a client, communicating about the work and the payment plan are key:

- Introduce yourself with a video conference or a phone call.
- Ask your client questions and brainstorm some solutions with them.
- Create a detailed outline of the work that will be done and have your client verify or add to it.

- Create and sign a contract before you begin work.
- Establish a limit to revisions to your work and your deadlines.
- Have a plan in place for unanticipated delays.
- Establish a secure payment method and timeframe for payment.
- Communicate clearly with your clients, asking questions or repeating information back to bring about clarity.
- Communicate often with your client, updating them on the progress.[21]

In some cases, your board will have the ability to fire you or will have control over your salary. Don't let that intimidate you. Remember that they are people, too, and establishing a trusting relationship with them will earn you the most credibility with them.

- Get to know the board members individually and build rapport.
- Don't embarrass your board members by your words or actions as a CEO. Your behavior reflects on them.
- Lead the board. Don't expect them to lead you. Hold the board accountable to the set standards of your business.
- Communicate clearly and regularly about what you need from the board.
- Don't talk about the board with your employees.
- Meet with each board member before the meeting to take care of important details and solve problems.
- Run your board meetings efficiently, only discussing the items together that cannot be resolved by one-on-one conversations with board members.
- Draft and send the board deck to board members before you meet. Align on important issues before each meeting.
- Tell them any bad news right away. Don't wait for a board

meeting.

- Don't be overrun by your board members. Stand your ground on critical issues.
- Make each board meeting productive and enjoyable. Be specific and to the point, while maintaining rapport.[22]

In addition to being efficient, you also need to be credible while working from home. Since your business doesn't have an official office building or storefront, you will need to find other ways to assure your team, your vendors, your clients, and your board that you're a professional, credible CEO. Use your confidence and professionalism to make people feel comfortable with both working with you and doing business with you.

Chapter 11 Key Takeaways

After reading this chapter, what should you understand?

1. Create a good workspace and get the equipment you need.
2. Make a zero-based plan to give every moment of the day a purpose.
3. Use communication and technology shortcuts for your team.
4. Guard your time and your space.
5. Use a daily huddle among your management team to communicate effectively and touch base each day.
6. Take care of your mental and physical health to be more effective.
7. Delegate tasks and focus on the most important ones yourself. Consider hiring a virtual assistant.
8. You need to communicate well and often with all parties you are working with to earn credibility.

Endnotes

1   Maria Cramer, Mihir Zaveri. "What if You Don't Want to

Go Back to the Office?" Accessed October 7, 2020. https://
www.nytimes.com/2020/05/05/business/pandemic-work-
from-home-coronavirus.html

2   "10 Productivity Stats That Will Surprise You." Accessed
September 3, 2020. https://www.workgroups.com/resou
rces/blog/10-productivity-stats-that-will-surprise-you/

3   "Working From Home: Balancing Productivity and
Well-Being." Accessed September 3, 2020. https://www.
mindtools.com/pages/article/working-from-home.htm

4   Christina Desmarais. "Get More Done: 18 Tips for
Telecommuters." Accessed September 3, 2020. https://
www.inc.com/christina-desmarais/get-more-done-18-tips-
for-telecommuters.html

5   "10 Productivity Stats That Will Surprise You." Accessed
September 3, 2020. https://www.workgroups.com/resou
rces/blog/10-productivity-stats-that-will-surprise-you/

6   "Results From New Study By UpRight In Partnership With
Ernst & Young Israel Link Posture And Productivity."
Accessed September 5, 2020. https://trainingindustry.com/
press-release/performance-management/results-from-new-
study-by-upright-in-partnership-with-ernst-young-israel-
link-posture-and-productivity/

7   Kayla Matthews. "10 Ways Posture Affects Productivity
(And How To Improve Both)." Accessed September 5, 2020.
https://www.asianefficiency.com/productivity/10-ways-
posture-affects-productivity-improve/

8   "1 in 3 adults don't get enough sleep." Accessed September
6, 2020. https://www.cdc.gov/media/releases/2016/p0215-
enough-sleep.html

9   "10 Productivity Stats That Will Surprise You." Accessed
September 3, 2020. https://www.workgroups.com/resou
rces/blog/10-productivity-stats-that-will-surprise-you/

10 "10 Productivity Stats That Will Surprise You." Accessed
September 3, 2020. https://www.workgroups.com/resourc

es/blog/10-productivity-stats-that-will-surprise-you/

11 Christina Desmarais. "Get More Done: 18 Tips for Telecommuters." Accessed September 3, 2020. https://www.inc.com/christina-desmarais/get-more-done-18-tips-for-telecommuters.html

12 "10 Productivity Stats That Will Surprise You." Accessed September 3, 2020. https://www.workgroups.com/resources/blog/10-productivity-stats-that-will-surprise-you/

13 "Multitasking Undermines Our Efficiency, Study Suggests." Accessed September 5, 2020. https://www.apa.org/monitor/oct01/multitask#:~:text=4)%20indicates%20that%20multitasking%20may,switches%20between%20the%20two%20tasks.

14 Timothy Ferriss. The 4-Hour Workweek. New York, Crown Publishers, 2007.

15 Tyler Basu. "How to Hire a Virtual Assistant: An Entrepreneur's Guide to Outsourcing & Hiring Virtual Staff." Accessed September 5, 2020. https://www.thinkific.com/blog/hire-a-virtual-assistant-outsourcing-guide/

16 Joel Trammell. "Why a CEO's Credibility Is More Fragile Than a Politician's Chances for Election." Accessed September 28, 2020. https://www.entrepreneur.com/article/273272

17 Lolly Daskal. "10 Powerful Ways You Can Earn Credibility in Your Industry." Accessed September 28, 2020. https://www.inc.com/lolly-daskal/10-powerful-ways-you-can-earn-credibility-in-your-industry.html

18 "11 Essential Tips for Managing Remote Employees." Accessed September 28, 2020. https://getlighthouse.com/blog/10-tips-manage-remote-employees/

19 Jason Aten. "7 Tips for Successfully Managing Remote Teams." Accessed September 28, 2020. https://www.inc.com/jason-aten/7-tips-for-working-fsuccessfully-

managing-remote-teams.html

20 Sue Poremba. "Vendor Management: 7 Tips for Security During Remote Work." Accessed September 28, 2020. https://securityintelligence.com/articles/vendor-management-remote-work/

21 Mindy Wagner. "10 tips for working with clients remotely: Part 1." Accessed September 28, 2020. https://www.webdesignerdepot.com/2009/03/10-tips-for-working-with-clients-remotely-part-1/

22 Mike Myatt. "Managing the Board: 10 Things Every CEO Should Know." Accessed September 28, 2020. https://www.n2growth.com/managing-board-relations/

Chapter 12

Speed It Up

Building your business does not have to be a process that takes many years. And for almost everyone, it's completely unrealistic for it to take this long. We have prepared you with ways to break down the insurmountable obstacles so you can get started, and do it fast. Think of the warp zones in old video games that allowed you to skip multiple levels and quickly get to the end and win. It's the same idea here. Our business shortcuts are in certain cases success fueled but they are in other cases because you may need to fail fast. Both in moving ahead successfully and in failing fast, you can realize shortcuts to get to the business finish line quickly.

The phrase 'time is money' is never so true as when you are setting out with your own business. You must adopt the mindset from the start to succeed in speeding things up. You must cut through a lot of fluff in your thinking and truly be disciplined in how you spend your time to create these warp zones to the finish line. For example, do you think you will attend the weekly in-person networking sessions that may come back in a post-COVID world? Maybe those sessions aren't that time efficient and you don't like small talk. In that case, cut them out. Do weekly one-on-one meetings with individual employees need to take an hour? Perhaps it's easier to have a 30-minute maximum on these meetings. Start to think deliberately about your time and how it is best spent.

We are going to split up our ways to get ahead fast into outward-focused and inward-focused efficiencies. Outward-focused efficiencies will be those focused on your audience. We have talked about sales and marketing but now you are going to think in warp zone speed about how to tackle audience penetration, and fast. Inward-focused efficiencies will be how you think about processes inside the business and inside your head.

Outward-Focused Efficiencies

Outward-focused efficiencies are ways that you can improve your growth for your audience. For outward-focused efficiencies, start by asking a few questions:

1. Who is my audience?
   - We have talked about your audience extensively but always start here.
2. Who is already important to them?
   - Examples include a news source, chamber of commerce, banker, lawyer, or social media influencer.
3. How can I get to my audience's influencers?
   - You can think about a call, email, in-person visit, or a gift to get their attention.
4. How can I maintain a solid relationship with the influencers to keep my audience buying and coming back?
   - Continue to offer something that the influencer can't say no to, that benefits your audience and you as well.

Let's go through a couple of examples. Jesse Itzler, a serial entrepreneur and the former CEO of Marquis Jet, relies on partnerships to grow quickly. He writes of his strategy at Marquis Jet in his social media feed, "Rather than trying to call 10,000 people one at a time to buy a jet card ... we realized that if we made one deal with Goldman Sachs they could email their 10,0000 qualified customers for us. It worked."[1]

A book author who was focused on selling to business owners decided to use an email list of chamber of commerce directors throughout the US to reach these business owners quickly. Within the email there was a suggestion for a potential event they could put together with a panel, questions for the moderator, and a link to the author's discounted book that could be given at the event.

Then there are franchises that are a part of a larger corporate entity. Let's say you're a gig owner CEO working on an element of the business for a franchisee. If you can succeed at exceeding expectations for one franchisee, this could result in more franchisees being brought on board. This could result in being asked to take over every element of the business element for all of the franchisees. Oftentimes, it just starts with a phone call, or an email, or a good idea in a conversation with friends.

Make Your Own Luck

Don't just rely on luck in hopes that you can get your business successful faster. Here are a few tips that can help you to make your own luck.

1. **Do what you know.** This really goes back to the idea of what type of business you want to run. You will find that when you do what you know, you are going to have a better success rate, and you will see your business pick up faster. After all, when you do what you know you are removing the process of learning a new trade or service. Also, be sure that you are doing what you love. When you love what you do, you are going to find that it is easier than ever to work a few extra hours or to push yourself a bit harder to make your business a success.
2. **Have a vision for the end result.** Be sure that you have a vision for what you want in the end. Working toward a vision will allow you to make the right decisions when needed to achieve this vision. For example, if you have a goal that within one year you can leave your regular job, then realize that each time you have an opportunity

to sell to a new client you need to take it. And you need to do a superb job in order to maintain this client for the future.

3. **Work at your strengths.** Make sure you are using your strengths to their fullest when working with the business. It is just as important to work on your weaknesses as well. If you are nervous when talking with new people, then practice and talk to more people to overcome this fear. And don't be afraid if you are not great at talking with new people at first; you will find that this is often comparable to public speaking and most people have an issue with it. The good news is the more you do it, the better you are going to become at presenting and networking.

4. **Set milestones that help you get to your end vision.** These milestones help set up smaller goals in order to hit your ultimate goal. And these milestones can be whatever works for you. For example, you may have a milestone to hire someone to work for you within six months; sign on a new client every six weeks; cultivate four repeat customers; etc. The list of milestones that you might have are endless, just cater the milestones toward your ultimate goals and your business model.

Keep learning and using what you learn to improve. An overall curiosity for getting better is the best way that you are going to grow your business at a quick speed. You can authentically claim that you are always learning and growing as the industry changes. This means so much to potential customers and is one way that you can ensure that your business grows as it should.

Tactics for Fast Growth

Knowing the answers to the questions mentioned earlier, as well as how to make your own luck, is just a small part of growing your business at a rapid rate. Here are proven methods that businesses throughout the world have used to quickly grow their business.

1. **Build a sales funnel.** A sales funnel can help a business scale and grow quickly. But, what should a sales funnel contain? Depending on your target of consumers or businesses and your sales cycle, you will create a sales funnel that makes the most sense. The idea is to find the funnel that is going to grow your business and fits your business needs.

2. **Have a CRM system.** Have a customer relationship management system (CRM) that is easy for you to use and means that you do not have to track the client transactions on your own, which is too time consuming. This goes back to having the right software on your end to help automate as much as possible.

3. **Research the competition.** Who is your competition? What are they doing? Take time to look at what they are doing and you can adopt what they do with some tweaks to make it your own. If your competition has seen a high success rate using a particular tactic, you can use a revised tactic to get your customers. And also keep a watchful eye on what they do so that you have the heads up as to whether you need to offer more, if your pricing is right, or if you need to make a new incentive.

4. **Have a customer loyalty program.** Once you have clients, make sure that you keep them. You can use a loyalty program to give people the incentive to still do business with you. For example, a business selling a product may offer discounts on their new product for loyalty members. Not only is this keeping customers with you, but it attracts more new customers since they may want these specific loyalty discounts.

5. **Always be looking for new opportunities.** If you see a need for a new offering, try to be the first company to offer it. When that is the case, you are naturally building the traction for your company. For example, a home business that offers homemade quilts, towels, etc., may have switched to providing face masks in the face of COVID. They saw the need for these products and how this could make them money.

6. **Build an email list.** One of the best ways to build an email list is with a landing page on your website where you offer something in order to get their email address. What is this free offer? It depends on your business. For example, those who offer a product may have a lead magnet set up for people to register their email address and get entered to win. Those who offer services may offer a small white paper meant to educate the customer. The ideas out there are endless.

7. **Leverage the platforms around you to succeed.** Depending on what industry your business falls into, you will find a lot of tech platforms that will help you grow. For example, a business that centers on ecommerce may find that Amazon's FBA service is what they need. If you are offering services, then consider Upwork to find clients that could use your service. These platforms allow people to leverage what they offer, whether this is a product or service, to get more clients and to be seen more.

Inward-Focused Efficiencies

The outward-focused efficiencies are without a doubt more important to your business getting ahead. But the inward-focused efficiencies are a close second and can slow down all of your other well-intentioned work and progress. Inward-focused efficiencies have to do with the habits of your business and of you, its leader. Let's look inside your business and your habits to make sure we have a finely tuned machine poised for growth.[2]

First, make sure to incentivize yourself and your team for newness. Be sure that your company culture fosters an environment where you are constantly questioning how you are spending time and money. Think about necessary meetings, strategy sessions, and company parties and how they work to create inward-focused efficiencies.

Next make sure you are creating a culture of spontaneity. Every business requires a level of creativity to surpass the competition. Cultivate spontaneity for yourself and your team by doing something different each week, month or quarter to exercise your mind and look at your business differently.

Ensure your business has a record of solid accounts receivable. Use a different software for credit cards, bill through a subscription, charge a fee if the bill comes in late, you name it to make sure that you get paid.

Next, simplify what you offer. Don't make anything, whether it's a product or process, too complicated.

And finally, delegate to the team. Don't feel like you are the only one who can do things. Hire an intern, hire a full-time person, get someone who can freelance and delegate the task so you can focus on larger issues and making yourself more creative.

Fail Fast, Fail Better

While we have talked about growing your business fast so that you start to see profit and growth, another important key to success is to fail fast. Sunnie Giles, founder of Quantum Leadership, writes, "Iterating fast failures achieves a desired result faster than perfecting the solution."[3] Our business environment continues to become more complex and, because of this, the speed of execution and continuous iteration is more important than perfect execution. Giles goes on to say, "A hallmark sign of today's effective leaders is his or her ability to unlearn old habits and change their mind when presented with convincing evidence."[4] Innovation needs failure as an ingredient and comfort with it is important.

Giles talks about failing fast in the same way that she talks about iterating and innovation. Turns out, they are intertwined. Failure should not be seen as an ugly word but something that must be confronted if you are to move forward quicker. Failing fast should not be mistaken for meaning to create things for the short term, but merely to take away the fear of failure and to eliminate anything that isn't working.

Think about your own habits at home and at work, and how you can change them to cultivate creativity and an ability to accept change and perhaps failure. We have a few suggestions. These ideas can allow for change, iteration, and speed to happen, whether you're successfully moving forward or failing fast to get to the next step.[5]

1. Shake up your normal routine. Drive a different way to normal places, change up your coffee shop, or change your hours.
2. Get to your deep work first, rather than reading the news or clearing out your inbox.
3. Experiment with ways to exercise your brain.
4. Become accustomed to laughing at yourself. Everything can be turned into a good story.

Failing fast and failing better is a mantra around iterating for positive and faster change in your business. Now let's address the reasons businesses fail, and fail for good. In analyzing these reasons, you can make a conscious decision to avoid these mistakes and perhaps even normalize them and be accepting of iteration. We have discussed the top three reasons but let's expand to see a bigger picture.[6]

1. There is no need for what they offer on the market
2. They ran out of cash
3. They had the wrong team working with them
4. They were out-competed
5. Pricing or cost issues
6. Product without a business model
7. Poor marketing
8. Lost focus
9. Pivot gone bad
10. Ignored customers

Knowing why businesses fail will hopefully eliminate ignorance, but you also need to think about the lessons we have gone through to ensure success. We know that it is essential to be willing and open to changing course. We have talked about doing the market research with a relentless focus and attention on the customer. Remember to stay financially lean so that a mistake doesn't mean that you can't keep iterating.

Before you start to feel as though the idea of starting your own business is full of failures lurking around the corner, remember that the research and hard work you have done thus far is going to help you avoid certain failures while making you unafraid of others. There is no need to hide from failure, but knowing that it is there can encourage you to work harder.

How to Pivot a Business

Pivoting a business is a term used to describe changing the course of a business to achieve better results. We saw a lot of pivots during COVID. For example, restaurants started focusing on curbside pickup and outdoor dining. Indoor gyms moved to backyards. And clothing factories started making personal protective equipment.

Once you know that a pivot is needed, the key is to stay resilient and focused when you start changing the business. You will find that the methods used to pivot a business successfully are very similar to how you should be ensuring your startup is a success. This means maintaining those new customers for the pivot that your business has done, as well as attracting new customers ... all things that were discussed in earlier chapters.

When should you pivot a business model? You don't want to pivot too soon, because it does take some time for things to get traction. However, if a pivot is needed and you don't do it, then chances are you will see your business suffer a financial fall. There are several signs that you can use that show you a pivot is needed.

Your first sign of needing a pivot is that your business will not show signs of growth or that it has hit a continuous plateau. While you are selling your product or service, you are not gaining new customers. If that is the case, take a look at what you are doing, what the employees of your company are doing and find a way to change. Perhaps you need to tweak your marketing strategy or product offering. In the most drastic cases, you might want to shift your entire business strategy altogether. You might find that the market is saturated with competition and this is making it harder to successfully reach your audience. In this case, you can look at other audiences or simplify your product offering to avoid the competition.

Here are some tips that businesses have used to make a pivot successful:

- Do it as soon as you can. Don't keep waiting for things to turn around, as the risk of waiting can use your time and money.
- Make sure that you spend time on new goals that are going to align with this new vision. Remember, when you pivot your business, you are going to be changing the end

goal, so the rest of the vision should line up accordingly.

- Reuse some aspects of the old business. There are going to be some aspects of your business that can be kept and reused with the new business idea.
- Listen to the customers and what they are saying. This is the only way to know if the pivot is really needed.

Growing your business is something that every CEO wants. The key to quick and continuous growth are the choices that you make. And above all else, remember it boils down to giving the customer what they want. Sara Blakely, who started Spanx, put it clearly when she stated: "Focus relentlessly on the person on the other side of the table."[7] Whether you are offering a product or a service, you should not be convincing your target market to buy what you are offering, you should be providing what they need.

Chapter 12 Key Takeaways

After reading this chapter, what should you understand?

1. There are outward-focused and inward-focused efficiencies that give your business huge advantages.
2. Develop partnerships and strategies with the influencers of your audience.
3. Simplify and delegate to make sure that inward-focused operations are running efficiently.
4. Don't be afraid of iteration and what it means to fail fast and fail better.

Endnotes

1 "Jesse Itzler." Accessed October 7, 2020. https://en.wikipedia.org/wiki/Jesse_Itzler

2 Elizabeth Walker, Ken Burgin. "16 Ways to Grow Your Business Without Spending Money." Accessed October 7,

2020. https://articles.bplans.com/17-ideas-you-can-steal-to-grow-your-business-without-spending-money/

3   Sunnie Giles. "How To Fail Faster – And Why You Should." Accessed October 7, 2020. https://www.forbes.com/sites/sunniegiles/2018/04/30/how-to-fail-faster-and-why-you-should/#31e04dd6c177

4   Sunnie Giles. "How To Fail Faster – And Why You Should." Accessed October 7, 2020. https://www.forbes.com/sites/sunniegiles/2018/04/30/how-to-fail-faster-and-why-you-should/#31e04dd6c177

5   Dom Price. "It's Time to Drop the 'Fail Fast' Mantra. Here's What Should Take It's Place." Accessed October 7, 2020. https://www.inc.com/dom-price/stop-trying-to-fail-fast-here-are-3-ways-to-fail-better.html

6   Stephanie Burns. "Why Entrepreneurs Fail: Top 10 Causes of Small Business Failure." Accessed October 7, 2020. https://www.forbes.com/sites/stephanieburns/2019/04/30/why-entrepreneurs-fail-top-10-causes-of-small-business-failure/#2585d7710200

7   Guest speaker at the 10x Growth Conference in Miami, FL. Feb 2019

Chapter 13

Run Your Business

It's now go time. You are ready and equipped to start, acquire or continue to run a business successfully from home. We have provided a no-nonsense look at the most important elements to get a successful business up and running. Whatever being a CEO from home looks like to you, make sure you enjoy the challenge. You have put in the time to create something special and a working lifestyle that is crafted to your needs.

As a residual owner CEO you might take over from previous owners as you acquire real estate, a blog, or another asset. A gig owner CEO might be launching their website and hiring experts in what they do. A traditional owner CEO might want to take a moment for a beta launch before introducing their new baby. Regardless of what type of CEO you are, read on to understand the nuances of a beta launch, the importance of studying analytics to make sure you're on the right track, and getting ready to scale, continue, or pivot your business.

Do a Soft Launch First

An effective way to start your business is to mentally prepare yourself for a soft launch. In the technology industry a soft launch has been referred to as a beta, for the various tests that software should go through (e.g., alpha, beta, etc.). A beta launch of your business is an early-release test run to see whether your product or service solves the problem you intended it to, is able to reach the group of people you intended, and to ensure that every aspect of your business runs smoothly.[1] A beta launch can help you succeed when you are ready for the final launch. It is a cost-effective way to test every part of your website, product, or service and make the necessary changes for the big day.

You may want to do a soft launch of your site by adding the word beta to your logo, while you continue to pursue customers and exposure for your site. Doing a beta launch has many benefits, including:

- Provide feedback so that you can fix bugs or performance issues that arise.
- Increase demand.
- Inform you whether people care about your product or if you need to tweak it or market it differently.
- Raise awareness of your company and product, building anticipation for the actual launch.[2]
- Allows you to gradually increase your customer base for sustainability and control.[3]
- Collect data to show to potential investors.
- Test your marketing plan.
- Get feedback on the cost and quality of your product.
- Become aware of additional competitors.
- Connect with beta testers.[4]

Attract Users and Gather Feedback

To have a successful soft launch, you need to attract users. You can attract beta users in a number of ways, including through websites such as BetaTesting.com if you need easy access to objective users. However, it can be more beneficial if you create your own email list of potential users/clients from subscribers through your website or your social media pages. You could even create a Facebook group or business page specifically for beta testing and use those networking skills you've been developing.

To gather feedback from your beta users, you'll need to provide incentive. You can offer prizes, discounts, or something to commemorate someone for being one of your users, such as listing them on a page on your website with a thank you.

Whatever you do, make sure you thank and demonstrate how much you value your beta user's feedback.[5]

Gather Feedback from Your Early Users

You'll want to be thorough in the information you gather from your beta users, while being respectful of their time. You'll want to ask them to:

- Report any issues they encounter in using your site, with payment, or the service they receive
- Suggest ways to improve your website or business
- Participate in the forums you provide where they can flag any issues, make suggestions, or provide additional feedback[6]

To analyze the feedback you receive, you'll need to weigh it against your expectations, the measurements you had previously decided on, and your expected outcomes. If you need a little help, there are plenty of tools out there to help you get started with your beta launch or to analyze the feedback you'll get.

HotJar
- Starts at $89/month
- Replay sessions of users on your website and find out what they look at, click on, and engage with
- Analyze data to make changes

BetaList
- Access a list of startups in the early, test stages
- Exchange feedback with other startups

BetaTesting
- Starts at $2,500 per project
- Get real user feedback

- Analyze results online

Erlibird
- Specific part of BetaTesting for Android, iOS, websites, desktop, and tech products
- Test for user experience, bugs, and usability

Betabound
- Post your startup to get beta testers funneled towards you
- Offer free test management resources
- Tester community for Centercode, a beta management company

Centercode
- Alpha testing helps find bugs and fix software based on a small group of testers.
- Beta testing tests your product in the market and produces product recommendations and insights from customers.
- Delta testing helps to get feedback as your product and business changes.

Testflight (Mobile)
- Allows you to beta test your app.
- Beta testers test your device on their iPhone, iPad, iPod touch, Apple Watch, and Apple TV.
- Invite 10,000+ users via email or a public link.
- Testers can take screenshots and send feedback immediately when an error occurs.[7]

BetaFamily
- An online community for beta testing for iOS and Android apps
- Filter testers by age, gender, nationality, and device
- Results from each test sent to you in a report[8]

Crashanalytics
- Helps pinpoint why an app crashed
- Can prioritize and fix issues
- Provides real-time alerts

You may want to check out some examples of companies that have well-designed beta programs to get some ideas for your own, such as the Apple Beta Software Program (https://beta. apple.com/sp/betaprogram/) and the Google Play Services Public Beta Program (https://developers.google.com/android/ guides/beta-program).

Get the Most Out of Your Soft Launch

To get the most out of your soft, or beta launch, you'll want to implement what you're learning along the way. If a customer or user brings a flaw in your product to your attention, get your team working on solving that issue right away. If you receive feedback about how to improve your checkout system, update it and see what customers think about the change. Be bold and experiment.

This is the time to fix all potential problems and improve your website, product, or service as much as possible. Make sure that as you do this, however, you are doing so with time limits, expectations, and measurable outcomes. Use the scientific model as a guide for this part of the process. You'll need to collect accurate data during this time to prepare you for your final launch.[9]

A Real-Life Success Story of a Beta Launch

Even if you aren't going to be launching the next tech unicorn, it's useful to understand how a beta launch works in real life. Let's take a look at an example of a startup with a successful beta launch. Eero (https://eero.com), a tech startup that offers non-traditional Wi-Fi for the home, attributes its success to their beta program. Their beta launch helped them refine their product and get the word out about their product early. They were able to test their hardware and software, making their guarantee for well-functioning Wi-Fi a promise backed by data.[10]

During their beta testing phase, Eero technicians were available around the clock, troubleshooting and assisting beta testers who had any issues with the Wi-Fi. This required Eero's entire management team to be on-board and prepared. They spent endless hours preparing for the beta launch, treating it as if it were the final launch.

The Eero management team handpicked beta testers who were referred to them by friends and family. They picked people who they felt would represent the diverse customer base they thought they would eventually have. They chose homes in different areas of the country, with different building materials and which had different kinds of devices that would be using their Wi-Fi. They even had a tester who wanted Wi-Fi in his treehouse.

Eero told these testers that they would be in touch with them twice a week with questions about the product and the process of the testing. They made sure their questions were open-ended and meant to draw out the most honest responses, such as if users had to change something about the product, what would it be.

The Eero management team decided it was time to launch when they knew they had a product and website that were functioning well enough that someone could reasonably use them. They knew they had some bugs and issues to work out still, but that was part of what the beta testing would help them do.

Eero had a six-month beta testing phase before they launched on a larger scale publicly. They made changes to their product and their process as issues arose. At the end of the beta process, just to be sure their product and process were in great shape, they brought on a group of brand-new beta users for fresh feedback. Their end time was determined by the timing of when they knew they had a product that was testing well in all cases. They had predetermined metrics which they had set out with the goal of meeting. When they met those, they knew it was time to move forward.[11]

Before their final, public launch, Eero spent quality time analyzing the feedback from their beta launch as a team. They used this time to work on communication between what the customer was saying the problem was and the engineers who would be addressing the issue in the final launch. They were able to get their communication flow between the team, the engineers, and the customers by communicating through Slack, a communication tool for teams.

The Eero team spent time thanking customers and letting them know how much they appreciated their participation. They found that all the time spent in communication with their testers made them loyal advocates of the brand. When it came to their final launch day, then, they had customers lined up to get their product.[12]

This book would not be complete without reiterating the word pivot. The word pivot is used in the tech industry to talk about a business shifting in a different direction. Be open to this concept and the importance of shifting your business if you determine in your beta launch (or at another point down the road) that you're not reaching your audience or are not meeting a need. When you launch an online business (or any business for that matter), you always want to be mindful of the areas you'll accrue the most revenue. Be open to "failing fast" and pivoting your concept if needed. It will save you money and time in the long run.

When you finish your beta phase, you will come out with compelling customer testimonials, investors, an improved site or product, or other benefits. Make sure you take the time to assess the process and what you've learned from it thoroughly. The learning should not stop there, however. You'll want to be prepared to assess your product, website, and business along the way. For that, you'll need some tools.

Using Analytics

It can be challenging to keep tabs on how performance is progressing across the board. Lucky for you, there's a wide assortment of analytics tools to help you gather important data to improve your website and business.

Analytics are the numbers that prove how well your business is running in terms of your marketing strategy, website, usability and demand for your product or business. These numbers are important because they provide you with valuable insights you can use to attract investors by showing them the numbers that prove you are a good investment, as well as help you keep tabs on real-time results and developing trends. These will enable you to continue to have success and to improve your business. You might be in the position where you will need to pivot your original concept to something else. You will need to use these analytics to pivot fast to a better solution.

If you're wondering what to track in analytics, consider looking at the following numbers and experimenting to see how you can improve them:

- New and returning visitors to your website
- Customers converting to sales
- Percentage of people who only visit once
- Traffic referred through other websites or social media
- Number of times advertisements are clicked versus seen (Click-through-rate)
- Visitors who get to website by clicking on an advertisement (Pay-per-click)

- Number of page views
- Time visitors spend on your site
- Amount customers spend per order (Average order value)[13]

Once you have launched your business, the behemoth for monitoring your site's usage is Google Analytics. This tool is free and allows you to track where and how people come to your site. If you're not sure where to start, you may want to try a 'how to' guide such as Moz's "Absolute Beginner's Guide to Google Analytics" (https://moz.com/blog/absolute-beginners-guide-to-google-analytics) or Google's own "Analytics Academy" (https://analytics.google.com/analytics/academy/course/6).

You will then be able to actively monitor new and returning customers, and track how many of your customers are converting to sales. Additionally, Google Analytics enables you to note important actions you've taken and the overall impact those actions have on the numbers.[14] You will be able to create reports which you can share with your team, such as audience reports, acquisition reports, behavior reports, and conversions. You can even use Google Analytics to track your social media campaigns.

You may also want to consider using Google Tag Manager and Google AdWords as well. Google Tag Manager is a tool that uses tags, or a short section of code added to a site, to collect data. It allows you to add, edit or disable tags on your site without having to work with the code. If you're not technologically inclined and don't have someone who is, this can be a great option for you. Even if you are, the Google Tag Manager can help you, with its "preview and debug" feature, which lets you test your tags before they're published to make sure they work. While it is best used in conjunction with Google Analytics, you could also use this with other analytics programs.[15]

Google AdWords is an advertising program where you place

a bid to have your ad featured in Google search results for specific keywords. It's free to create and account, but you have to pay every time someone clicks on one of them, based on the bid you placed. You'll want to use keywords that people might actually use and that are actually relevant to your website, but highly competitive keywords will cost more because others will be bidding on them, too. Google AdWords can be a great help in your final launch, used in conjunction with Google Analytics, but keep in mind that, on average, small businesses spend $9,000 to $10,000 on Google Ads per month.[16]

Google Search Console helps you measure the traffic to your site from searches and your site's performance in searches. You can also use it to fix issues and make them more findable. You can get useful information from it such as which search queries are bringing people to your site, what the search engine ranking is, and how many clicks it's getting. It will email you alerts when you need to fix an issue on your site and provide information about the crawl, serving information and index of your page.[17]

Other Analytics Tools to Consider
While Google Analytics may be the go-to option for most businesses, it isn't the only viable option on the market. Take a look at some of these others to decide if they would better serve your purposes.

Kissmetrics
- Understand customer behavior with tracking and analyzing tools
- Prices start at $500 a month
- Get information about where people drop off the funnel and which channels bring in the most revenue[18]

Crazy Egg
- Provides heatmaps and confetti reports

- Records individual sessions
- Includes A/B split testing to compare variations of your page
- Enables you to change your website content with their editing tools

Chartio
- Cloud-based analytics tool
- Compare data from various business applications
- Connects all your databases
- Create and share visualizations of the data with your team

Appsee
- Tracks all actions of app users in real time
- Replay videos of user sessions
- Automatically shows you problems in your app and how to fix them
- Collects all data into reports
- Has a free version you can use in your beta phase[19]

Applying Analytics Feedback

Some of the analytics tools allow you to apply what you are learning right away. Most likely, you'll need to use them to give you a meta-perspective to inform your approach. For this, you'll want to place the most emphasis on whoever provides funding for the website, be it the customers who are coming to your website to buy a product or a group of companies who are paying for the attention or information from a group of users on your site. How can you get the revenue numbers higher?

As you problem-solve how to do this, remember to direct the user or customer to the area of your website that drives the most revenue, through calls to action and links. Use great copy to drive customers to a cart to check out, and make the process as easy as possible. If you want to hold the users' attention, be sure to direct them towards deeper content with persuasive hooks so that they spend more time on your site.

Scale, Maintain, or Pivot

It's every business owner's dream to become an overnight success. Most likely this won't happen and you also might not wish for it. If you grow faster than you are prepared for, it will result in major issues. In fact, 74% of startups that fail are at least in part because of premature scaling.[20] The fact is that you will be looking at three options: scaling a business quickly, maintaining your business with reasonable growth, or pivoting your business. Let's talk about the fun option of scaling first.

To prepare to scale, make sure your product or service is in the best shape possible. You don't want to mass-produce something that's flawed. You should have already checked for errors in your beta launch, but if you haven't implemented all the necessary changes, you'll want to do so now.

Check your resources. Do you have accessibility to funding, supplies, manufacturing, or new hires if needed? Perform your due diligence and make sure every aspect of your business is set up to run smoothly, from a marketing plan to internal business organization to the hiring and on-boarding process for new employees.

Make yourself a manager in the background of your company. Here's where you'll know that you are ready to scale, when your business can run without you. That means, if you need to take a sick day you could and your business wouldn't suffer for it. This means your team needs to be working well together, running every aspect of the business as smoothly as possible.

The option of maintaining your business with a slight upturn or downturn is the next option and is fairly straightforward. You need to constantly be searching for trends that are long term or short term so you can make sure to decipher whether your business is in trouble and needs to pivot or can sustain itself as it is. You can use the analytics we have discussed and the marketing tips to help with your sales and marketing process.

Finally, you may need to consider a pivot for your business. As we have discussed, the worst thing you can do is not to fail, but to fail too slowly that you eat up your runway, or the resources that you have to launch your business. It is easier said than done, but if you can nimbly move in a different direction with your business you will be better for it in the long run.

Enjoy the Ride

You may think you can launch or run your business and let your advertising and network do the hard work for you. It's critical to stay in the game. The launch is just the beginning and even though it feels like you have been running the race for a while, you are merely crossing the start line. This is the time when small businesses either lose some of the momentum they had originally gained in their launch or become overrun by unexpected success and find that they can't handle to continue a healthy level of customer engagement while they're scrambling to meet the demand.

You will want to identify the long-term goals for you and your business. Do you want to continue running the business from home indefinitely? Do you want to pass your business down to family members? Do you want it to lead to philanthropic work? Do you want it to lead to an expertise that you can develop to either write, teach, or do board work? You should create some ideas for what you would like this work to hold for you in your future.

Running a company as a CEO is not just about a title, it is about operating a successful business. It is going to be hard. There are going to be times that you doubt what you are doing and your abilities. However, if you stick with it, and use the tools you have developed, you will find success. Good luck in launching, building, and growing your business and welcome to the freedom of being your own boss, of being a CEO from home.

Chapter 13 Key Takeaways
After reading this chapter, what should you understand?

1. Do a soft launch first to uncover critical errors.
2. Have a reliable analytics tool (or two) in place before your official launch to monitor how your business is doing.
3. Think about the three outcomes of your business, which will be to scale, maintain or pivot, and be prepared for each outcome.
4. Identify the long-term goals of your work and your business so it carries more significance for you.

Endnotes

1   Craig Strong. "Launching & Learning — A Beta Release." Accessed April 27, 2020. https://medium.com/the-lean-product-lifecycle/launching-learning-a-beta-release-37f73ba4ac06
2   "Beta Launch: Release a feature-complete product, but with known or unknown bugs." Accessed April 27, 2020. http://learningloop.io/plays/beta-launch
3   Varsha Agrawal. "Why Beta launch is essential for every startup?" Accessed April 27, 2020. https://blog.betapage.co/why-beta-launch-is-essential-for-every-startup-f02cd4deffb9
4   Varsha Agrawal. "Why Beta launch is essential for every startup?" Accessed April 27, 2020. https://blog.betapage.co/why-beta-launch-is-essential-for-every-startup-f02cd4deffb9
5   "Beta Launch: Release a feature-complete product, but with

known or unknown bugs." Accessed April 27, 2020. http://
learningloop.io/plays/beta-launch

6   "Beta Launch: Release a feature-complete product, but with
known or unknown bugs." Accessed April 27, 2020. http://
learningloop.io/plays/beta-launch

7   "Beta Testing Made Simple with TestFlight." Accessed April
30, 2020. https://developer.apple.com/testflight/

8   "Find and engage app testers." Accessed April 30, 2020.
https://betafamily.com

9   Craig Strong. "Launching & Learning — A Beta Release."
Accessed April 27, 2020. https://medium.com/the-lean-
product-lifecycle/launching-learning-a-beta-release-
37f73ba4ac06

10 "The Beta Program Behind This Startup's Winning Launch."
Accessed April 27, 2020. https://firstround.com/review/the-
beta-program-behind-this-startups-winning-launch/

11 "The Beta Program Behind This Startup's Winning Launch."
Accessed April 27, 2020. https://firstround.com/review/the-
beta-program-behind-this-startups-winning-launch/

12 "The Beta Program Behind This Startup's Winning Launch."
Accessed April 27, 2020. https://firstround.com/review/the-
beta-program-behind-this-startups-winning-launch/

13 Beatriz Estay. "Measuring Success: Analytics." Accessed
April 27, 2020. https://www.bigcommerce.com/blog/
measuring-online-success/#key-performance-indicators-
kpis-to-include-in-your-online-marketing-strategy

14 Beatriz Estay. "How to Create, Setup, and Launch a
Profitable Online Store (Seriously)." Accessed April 27,
2020. https://www.bigcommerce.com/blog/how-to-create-
online-store/#launching-your-online-store

15 Angela Petteys. "An Introduction to Google Tag Manager."
Accessed April 29, 2020. https://moz.com/blog/an-
introduction-to-google-tag-manager

16 "What Is Google AdWords? How the Google Ads Auction

Works." Accessed April 29, 2020. https://www.wordstream.com/articles/what-is-google-adwords

17 "Google Search Console." Accessed April 29, 2020. https://search.google.com/search-console/about

18 "The 8 Best Analytics Tools For Startups." Accessed April 30, 2020. https://www.feedough.com/startup-resources/the-8-best-analytics-tools-for-startups/

19 "The 8 Best Analytics Tools For Startups." Accessed April 30, 2020. https://www.feedough.com/startup-resources/the-8-best-analytics-tools-for-startups/

20 Neil Patel. "7 Ways to Prepare Your Startup to Scale Up." Accessed April 30, 2020. https://www.inc.com/neil-patel/7-ways-to-prepare-your-startup-to-scale-up.html

About the Authors

Jennifer Morehead is an entrepreneur, sales and marketing expert, independent board member, private investor, and fundraiser. She successfully founded Salesboxer, which provides marketing solutions for local businesses throughout the country, and sold the business to her co-author Heather Sallee. She is currently the CEO of Flex HR, which provides outsourced human resources solutions to companies throughout the country.

Heather Sallee is the CEO of Salesboxer. Throughout her career, she has worked with companies in the initial stages of their marketing journey and also with well-established companies that needed to overcome negative reviews. With Salesboxer, she provides written content for blogs, emails, and social media posts to help create an image that is up front, positive, and informative for each client's target demographic.

BUSINESS
BOOKS

Business Books

Business Books publishes practical guides
and insightful non-fiction for beginners and professionals.
Covering aspects from management skills, leadership and
organizational change to positive work environments, career
coaching and self-care for managers, our books are a valuable
addition to those working in the world of business.

15 Ways to Own Your Future
Take Control of Your Destiny in Business and in Life
Michael Khouri
A 15-point blueprint for creating better collaboration, enjoyment, and success in business and in life.
Paperback: 978-1-78535-300-0 ebook: 978-1-78535-301-7

The Common Excuses of the Comfortable Compromiser
Understanding Why People Oppose Your Great Idea
Matt Crossman
Comfortable compromisers block the way of anyone trying to change anything. This is your guide to their common excuses.
Paperback: 978-1-78099-595-3 ebook: 978-1-78099-596-0

The Failing Logic of Money
Duane Mullin
Money is wasteful and cruel, causes war, crime and dysfunctional feudalism. Humankind needs happiness, peace and abundance. So banish money and use technology and knowledge to rid the world of war, crime and poverty.
Paperback: 978-1-84694-259-4 ebook: 978-1-84694-888-6

Mastering the Mommy Track
Juggling Career and Kids in Uncertain Times
Erin Flynn Jay
Mastering the Mommy Track tells the stories of everyday working mothers, the challenges they have faced, and lessons learned.
Paperback: 978-1-78099-123-8 ebook: 978-1-78099-124-5

Modern Day Selling
Unlocking Your Hidden Potential
Brian Barfield
Learn how to reconnect sales associates with customers and unlock hidden sales potential.
Paperback: 978-1-78099-457-4 ebook: 978-1-78099-458-1

The Most Creative, Escape the Ordinary, Excel at Public Speaking Book Ever
All the Help You Will Ever Need in Giving a Speech
Philip Theibert
The 'everything you need to give an outstanding speech' book, complete with original material written by a professional speechwriter.
Paperback: 978-1-78099-672-1 ebook: 978-1-78099-673-8

On Business And For Pleasure
A Self-Study Workbook for Advanced Business English
Michael Berman
This workbook includes enjoyable challenges and has been designed to help students with the English they need for work.
Paperback: 978-1-84694-304-1

Small Change, Big Deal
Money as if People Mattered
Jennifer Kavanagh
Money is about relationships: between individuals and between communities. Small is still beautiful, as peer lending model, micro-credit, shows.
Paperback: 978-1-78099-313-3 ebook: 978-1-78099-314-0

Readers of ebooks can buy or view any of these bestsellers
by clicking on the live link in the title. Most titles are published
in paperback and as an ebook. Paperbacks are available in
traditional bookshops. Both print and ebook formats
are available online.
Find more titles and sign up to our readers' newsletter at
http://www.jhpbusiness-books.com/
Facebook: https://www.facebook.com/JHPNonFiction/
Twitter: @JHPNonFiction